Juvenile Offenders in Victorian Lancashire

W.J. Garnett and the Bleasdale Reformatory

by
Emmeline Garnett

Centre for North-West Regional Studies
Lancaster University
2008
Series Editor: Jean Turnbull

Juvenile Offenders in Victorian Lancashire: W.J. Garnett and the Bleasdale Reformatory

This volume is the 55th in a series of Occasional Papers published by the
Centre for North-West Regional Studies at the University of Lancaster

Text Copyright © Emmeline Garnett 2008

Designed, typeset, printed and bound by
4word Ltd, Bristol

British Library Cataloguing in-Publication Data
A CIP catalogue entry for this book is available from the British Library

ISBN 978-1-86220-214-6

Contents

Abbreviations

LRO   Lancashire Record Office

GA   Gloucestershire Archives

List of Illustrations

Acknowledgements

To my niece Carol Johnson for lending me the diaries of William James Garnett and William Garnett without which the book could not have been written. To Angus Winchester for being interested in the project from its inception and for taking the photographs. To the Centre for North-West Regional Studies for their usual meticulous work on the production. To Michael Derbyshire and Michael Winstanley for help with bits that needed more knowledge of computers than I possess. To Sandra Jolly for drawing my attention to her Ph.D. thesis on Lancashire Reformatories. To Jean Fone for her enthusiastic knowledge of Bleasdale history. To Muriel Lord for local information and photographs 12 and 13. To Jeremy Duckworth, Beryl Owers, Iris Westcott and Christine Whitehead for personal information regarding the reformatory.

CHAPTER ONE

The Growth of 'Juvenile Delinquency'

Juvenile delinquency did not exist as a concept until the end of the eighteenth century, and according to the *Oxford English Dictionary* the phrase itself was not invented until 1815, when a committee of concerned philanthropists was convened 'for Investigating the Alarming Increase of Juvenile Delinquency in the Metropolis.' The idea grew and spread:

> In the eighteenth century, juveniles were rarely indicted in the courts and contemporaries did not usually regard them as a separate or particularly threatening problem. By the mid-nineteenth century, juvenile delinquency was established as a major focus of anxiety among the propertied.[1]

Many arguments have been put forward to account for this, none of them entirely satisfactory, but changes in the social background of the country, as well as its intellectual landscape, clearly had a strong bearing on the situation. The greatest change was the industrial revolution. This had far-reaching repercussions for the whole population, but those at the bottom of the social scale were hardest hit, with fewer resources to enable them to cope with the changes. Rapid urbanisation and industrialisation resulted in the situations most graphically portrayed by Engels in his *The Condition of the Working Class in England*, first published in 1844.

At the same time the idea of childhood was developing – childhood as a separate world, and children as something other than merely undeveloped adults. *Oliver Twist*, published in 1837, brought the world of juvenile destitution and juvenile crime forcibly to the public eye, but the book is perhaps even more interesting as the first English novel in which the protagonist was a child and remained a child to the last chapter.

The perception of childhood as separate, not easy to understand, and therefore in some ways to be feared, was similar to a more recent perception of the teenage years. The new urban populations tended to be young and, as the first half of the century progressed, the magistrates' courts, and beyond them the middle-class public at large, felt swamped by a tide of unruly and vicious youngsters, against whose depredations they had no effective response. Not all were criminals in the accepted sense, for many were merely beggars and vagrants, but the effect on the respectable part of society was the same. There was at the time a very real fear of a breakdown in the whole underlying framework of law and order. The French Revolution may not have been responsible for its inception but the wind of change blowing from across the Channel kept the smouldering tinder in a constant glow. At the same time the sense of property was of ever-increasing importance to the middle classes.

In many ways efforts to cope exacerbated the problem. It has been argued that 'by criminalising forms of juvenile behaviour previously ignored by the courts, parliament legislated juvenile delinquency into existence'[2] and the new police forces, backed by the courts, formed, in the words of a contemporary writer, a 'gigantic and indiscriminate agency for the supposed suppression of crime.'[3] Numbers of children were arrested for 'crimes' of petty larceny for which adults, or indeed young offenders from a different class, would have been more lightly treated:

> Robbing orchards or henroosts is regarded only as a clever feat in the gentleman's son at a public school, and while a boy who steals lead from the top of a house is threatened with transportation for the next offence, stealing knockers from the door by a young student is considered a spirited feat, to be punished, if at all, only by a fine and a reprimand.[4]

Some observers saw the tendency and regretted it. Thomas Barwick Lloyd-Baker, founder of one of the earliest reformatories, observed with a typical lightness of touch in a letter to a newspaper, referring to some magistrates' sentences he had met:

> No 1. 11-years-old — cutting off a branch of a laurel hanging over a lane, 3 years. No 2. Using very bad language to a donkey, 3 years. Nos. 3 and 4, ages 10 and 14 — highway robbery. A small boy had been sent to buy three pennyworth of sugar, and passing nos. 3 and 4 in the village street, they hustled him down and ate up the sugar. Very wrong, I grant; but not a case of pistols on Hounslow.[5]

Whether they hankered for the good old days or not, many magistrates were increasingly frustrated by the limited scope which they had in dealing with young offenders. They could be handed back into the care of their parents, but in many cases the home background was seen to be at the root of the problem. This apart, there was nothing but jail, followed by transportation, and although the situation in the country's prisons had been slowly improving ever since John Howard's pioneering work in the 1770s, it took no formal account of the age of the wrong-doer. Children of any age over seven years were sent down for steadily increasing periods as they reappeared time and again in the dock. In prison, even the most basic steps to prevent youngsters from hardening into a life of crime were not always possible. As the nineteenth century advanced, some newly-built prisons allowed for separate accommodation for juveniles, but there were still plenty of old prisons. As late as 1847 it was reported that in Newgate, with an annual population of 3,000, of whom 400 were boys under 16, there was daytime segregation, but at night the wards were mixed, and locked without light from five in the evening to seven the next morning.[6]

The system of transportation had commenced in 1787 and finally came to an end in 1868, by which time nearly 160,000 sentences had been carried out. After 1841, though, the writing was on the wall, and this sharpened the debate as to what could be done to solve the problem of juvenile offenders. Many magistrates and others were deeply concerned at the situation as they watched juveniles coming through the revolving doors of the courts until they grew and hardened into full-blown criminals.

The first experiments towards a remedy, as was normal in all social fields in the nineteenth century, came from private philanthropy. One of the earliest figures in the field was Edward Brenton (1774–1839), who did not differentiate between delinquency and destitution. By 1813, after a naval career highlighted by some daredevil exploits, he had been laid up in the depressing dry dock of 'half-pay', and the navy never called on him again. He turned to philanthropy, took an interest in the temperance movement and the relief of shipwrecked sailors, and found an outlet for his concern for his fellow man in the foundation of 'The Society for the Suppression of Juvenile Vagrancy', later rechristened by the snappier title of 'The Children's Friend Society'. This organisation concentrated on training boys to earn their own living by manual labour, and then sent them abroad. They trained 700 boys in total over the years, and most were sent to the Cape Colony. It is probable that Brenton's character, stronger in the heart than the head, had much to do with the society's ensuing troubles. He failed to foresee the possible problems of emigration, or to take sufficient care about the placing of his boys and their later superintendence. Allegations of abuse and virtual slavery led to a public enquiry in Cape Colony, and this may well have hastened Brenton's sudden death. The society's doubtful reputation caused it to be starved of philanthropic funding, and it folded only three years later in 1842. However, whatever its troubles, it had pioneered a path which increasing numbers of influential people would tread.[7]

In its earlier and happier years, Brenton's society had some powerful supporters, including the Hon. Amelia Matilda Murray (1795–1884), whose mother was a lady-in-waiting at the court of George III. Together Brenton and Miss Murray founded the girls' home of the Children's Friend Society in Chiswick, and the Murray family's high social profile was extremely useful in giving publicity to this new branch of philanthropic effort. This did not, however, save the original society from closure.

Mary Carpenter (1807–1877) was a remarkable educationalist who has been insufficiently regarded, partly through her own fault (she refused to address the first conference she was instrumental in convening as it was not becoming in a woman). The daughter of a Bristol Unitarian minister, she and her sisters initially ran a small girls' school, but she raised her sights to the: 'enormity and amount of juvenile depravity' and its 'appalling progress, in a ratio far exceeding that of the population generally.'[8] By the 1840s, when Government was becoming involved, she was much consulted, and her book published in 1851 and rather quaintly called *Reformatory Schools for the Children of the Perishing and Dangerous Classes* was a powerful influence in the raising of public and political concern which resulted in the 1854 'Act for the better care and reformation of youthful offenders in Great Britain.' This opened the way to the whole reformatory movement. For her, the 'perishing' classes were those who were in immediate danger of being converted to a life of crime 'from their ignorance, destitution and the circumstances in which they are growing up.'[9] The 'dangerous' classes were those who had crossed the divide and were already branded as criminals.

Widely cognizant of the available literature, which chiefly consisted of the reports of a small number of enlightened prison governors and chaplains such as the Reverend John Clay of Preston, and increasingly called upon as an adviser, she had also plenty of hands-on experience, having opened her first Ragged School in Bristol in 1846. In her earlier years she had learnt how to teach in a number of practical situations, beginning by working in her father's boys' school at the age of 15, and although it was not in her nature to be scathing, she was very clear-eyed about the failures of those benevolent institutions which tried to run on religion and goodwill without, on the one hand, a real respect for the children, and, on the other, a practical knowledge of how to interact with them.

Mary Carpenter's book contained statistics, official reports and individual examples and presented a picture of the situation as it existed, describing in some detail the three-pronged solution which was emerging: Free Day Schools, Industrial Feeding Schools, and Reformatory Schools – the three dealing with the problem at increasingly serious and refractory levels.

Free Day Schools developed out of the Ragged School movement, which were largely evening and Sunday institutions. They accepted the children whose levels of cleanliness and clothing made them unacceptable to the more respectable poor – those who found the pennies necessary to send their children to ordinary day-schools. The movement had been started by Robert Raikes in 1781, and had spread widely in the cities, fostered by people of undoubted goodwill but often, as Mary Carpenter pointed out, with hopelessly inadequate resources both financial and human:

> Since these Schools are conducted solely through the medium of moral and religious influence, it is clearly necessary to secure a large enough amount of this to obtain absolute control over the hitherto unsubdued material that is to be wrought upon. We have not here the aids, so important in other Schools, of an established discipline, which of itself imposes considerable check on children ...... A number of wild and generally vicious children assemble together, for an object which many of them cannot understand, without any effective curb on their wildness and violence, without any authority, as yet acknowledged and established, to subdue them.[10]

She quoted lurid passages from the reports of helpless would-be teachers drowning in uncontrollable tides. None-the-less, her summing up was that the movement had been valuable, not only in the number of children it had undoubtedly influenced for the better, but in a change in the relationship between the classes at the top and bottom of society:

> There may have been much that was unnecessary, much that was unwise in what has been done, and the manner of doing it; but it has tended to establish the practical conviction that we are all of one human family, and that, as such, the strong ought to try to help the weak.[11]

Mary Carpenter described in detail one successful Free Day School for such children in Bristol. This was the only one favourably reported on in a report of 1850 to the Committee of Council on Education[12] and it was the one she established herself. The basis of the school and its teaching, were, as one would expect at this period, heavily reliant upon religion, but the list of rules which her committee drew up has two significant clauses. One was that although: 'The fundamental principles of religion, in which all professed Christians agree, shall form the basis of the instruction given' yet 'All sectarian theology shall be carefully avoided.' The other is more surprising, given the received wisdom of the time: 'No corporal punishment, or holding up to shame or ridicule, shall be made use of, but discipline must be maintained by the Master's own firmness, order and kindness.'

Clearly she had recruited a quite remarkable master and his wife who ran the school between them, but she also imputed much of its success to the industrial training given. Two hours a day were given to sewing for the girls, tailoring and shoemaking for the boys, work which disciplined the children and paid them, allowing them to save small amounts of money as part of their education. Moreover, she was a firm believer in the value of recreation, in which she included music: 'We need only observe the attraction presented by a street singer to the children that crowd around, to be fully assured that music may have a most powerful influence over the wild and refractory.'[13]

The main impediment, apart from a constant shortage of money which had to be raised entirely from well-wishers, was the short span of time which most children spent in school. The numbers on the books bore little relation to the numbers in attendance at any one time, and the figures showed that those who came for no more than a month were in the vast majority.

The so-called Industrial Feeding Schools seem to have originated with Sheriff Watson of Aberdeen in 1841. It had been estimated that the county had over 1,000 beggars and vagrants preying on the settled population, and that a third of these were children.[14] An Industrial School was set up to accept children for a 12-hour day, during which they would be given three meals, school lessons and industrial training – typically laundry and sewing for girls, tailoring and shoemaking for boys. The police were instructed to apprehend all child beggars and bring them in. The system worked as far as it went – the streets of Aberdeen were spectacularly cleared of beggars – but how far the problem was merely displaced is hard to calculate. As with the Ragged Schools, the chief problem for all Industrial Schools was the mobility of the children for whom they were designed, and until 1854 the fundamental problem remained the same – the prisons were the only establishments which had any legal power of detention.

If child criminals were to be given the chance of reformation, the establishments to do the work could not expect real success until government provided a legal sanction, which was slow in coming. France was ahead in this. M. Demetz's establishment at Mettrai outside Tours took juveniles from prison to finish their sentence and had the power to enforce attendance, but in fact operated an open-door system which was hardly ever abused. It kept children in small groups with housefathers who lived, worked and played alongside their 'family'. Staffing was generous and the discipline minute, with an ascending scale of punishments, the ultimate of which was return to prison. Corporal punishment, however, was absolutely prohibited, and the system worked.

Mettrai had a very powerful effect on the movement in England, perhaps most obviously in the foundation by the Philanthropic Society of their farm school at Redhill. Sydney Turner, chaplain to the Society and first principal at Redhill, visited Mettrai in 1846 and found that of the 500 inmates since its foundation, 144 had so far been sent out into the world to monitored workplaces, and of these an impressive 85 per cent were conducting themselves satisfactorily.

Sydney Turner (1814–1879), had worked for the Philanthropic Society since 1840 as its resident chaplain and superintendent of the Institution in Southwark. The Society started work among destitute children as early as 1788, saving them from the streets and teaching them a trade. Already considering how this work could be adapted to new perceptions, particularly to the perceived separation of destitution from delinquency, Turner was profoundly influenced by his visit to Mettrai. He persuaded his society that modern social problems would best be dealt with by moving the establishment into the country.[15]

One feature of the early reformatory movement was the almost universal belief in the salutary effects of outdoor physical labour allied to a suitable moral environment. In 1848 it was agreed to buy a 133-acre farm at Redhill in Surrey, and the Farm School opened in 1849. At that time, the place had to be run on voluntary lines, but once the Act of 1854 was passed, the voluntary principle was phased out, as Redhill and all other reformatories realised that it simply did not work to include some voluntary inhabitants among those sent by the courts. Sydney Turner was appointed the first Superintendent and Chaplain at Redhill, so that by the time the Act was passed he had probably more hands-on experience of reformatory work than anyone in the country. His own philosophy was expressed in his 1846 report to the Society:

> Voluntary, not enforced good conduct must be the object we aim at; for this alone will last. If we render the boy dependent on the superintendence and discipline which we subject him to, he will be but as a child needing strings; and when the artificial support which he has been used to leaning upon is necessarily withdrawn on his going forth into the world, he will be liable to fail at every step he takes in life.[16]

In England the first purpose-built foundation with the power of the law behind it was Parkhurst on the Isle of Wight. This was an establishment which took young criminals who had been sentenced to transportation, with the object of training them before they were sent abroad. If the training was successful, the transportation sentence could be rescinded, with the result that the place was heavily used by magistrates who saw it as by far the lesser of two evils, and the 320 places were rapidly filled and kept filled. Its methods were strongly influenced by the jail system from which it sprang rather than the real philanthropy of the private institutions. It opened in 1838 and in the first eight years 1,200 boys were sent there.

The Parkhurst system relied on segregation – even the schoolroom was partitioned into little cells, so that 'the Schoolmaster can inspect and instruct without the possibility of the boys communicating with or seeing each other.' The *Illustrated London News*, in an article of 1847, summed it up: 'A visit to Parkhurst prison .... is one of the most gratifying scenes of philanthropy to be enjoyed in this great Christian country.'[17] However, in the same year the governor was reporting, rather wearily, that 'there has not been that evidence of a general and growing desire to improve in moral conduct and industrial energy which I anxiously looked for, and the apparent absence of which causes me much disappointment.' Mary Carpenter, quoting this, remarked with unusual asperity that her readers:

> will feel no surprise that the governor's hopes are unfulfilled, not it may be through any fault of his own, but through the radical error of the whole system. It attempts to fashion children into machines instead of self-acting beings, to make them obedient prisoners within certain iron limits, not men who have been taught how to use their liberty without abusing it.'[18]

Parkhurst closed in 1869.

Once the idea of juvenile reformatories took hold in the national imagination, it moved with such speed that it is difficult to unravel the order of events. There is no simple chronological order of what, or who, wielded the influence, but an immensely important figure was Thomas Barwick Lloyd-Baker (1807–1886). The only son of a rich Gloucestershire squire, Lloyd-Baker's upbringing and interests were predictable. He went to Eton and Oxford, inherited and ran the family estates, and became a magistrate and visiting justice to the county prisons. In many ways a typical country squire, with all the sporting and social interests of his class, he was a man with a deep sense of the responsibilities of privilege. A German visitor remarked with astonishment that he probably spent three days a week in unpaid public service.

Gloucestershire jails were already famous for being run on the most modern lines. Sir George Onesiphorus Paul (1746–1820), a magistrate, chairman of the Grand Jury and High Sheriff, had been mainly responsible for a private Act of Parliament in 1791 which allowed Gloucestershire to rebuild all its jails. Segregation to avoid contamination was the watchword, but although segregation of the sexes was satisfactorily carried out, and segregation by type of offence (debtors separate from criminals, those on remand from the convicted), segregation by age, which Paul favoured, was considered too expensive, and was still not achieved when Lloyd-Baker became a magistrate in 1833.

At the same time, Gloucestershire's population was growing rapidly, and Cheltenham had particular problems. Its population, some 3,000 in 1801, had by 1841 risen to over 31,000, added to which it received many thousands of middle-class visitors every year. It is not surprising that it had more than its share of predatory hangers-on.[19] In the 1840s there were more young thieves convicted in Cheltenham than in the rest of the county put together.[20] Lloyd-Baker began thinking about juvenile reformation quite early in his career, but, as so often happens, the

From a drawing by G.Richmond Esq.r R.A.

1: Thomas B Lloyd-Baker. Reproduced by permission of Gloucester Archives. Ref D3549/25/8/27.

defining moment appeared to arrive quite haphazardly. In 1836, he was in a group of people playing a party game of guessing characteristics from handwriting. His attention was attracted by the piece handed to him, which was a few lines on the subject of reforming young offenders. When he commented on the subject-matter, the writer swept him into a corner and they talked for two hours.

> The lady was Miss Murray and when a fortnight later she returned up to London I went to see her and she shewed me the Girls' Reformatory at Chiswick .... She also introduced me to poor Captain Brenton who had some years before commenced a boys' Reformatory which was working at Hackney.[21]

The next year Lloyd-Baker was already drawing a plan for a reformatory, and sent it for comment to Edward Brenton, who responded that he did not think that the Poor Law Commissioners, 'thickheaded, obstinate, illiterate and unfeeling'[22] would endorse it. Lloyd-Baker continued to think about reformatories for the next ten years as he conscientiously served his stint as a magistrate (it was said that he never missed a Quarter Session in his life).

> but saw myself no nearer to it ....The work required some man who would give himself up to it heart and soul, with a determination to carry it through. I was fully occupied with the work into which it had pleased God to put me, and I had no right to give that up for what everybody except myself believed to be a mere crotchet.[23]

The breakthrough came in 1851, when Lloyd-Baker met George Bengough (1828–1865), a young man from a prosperous Gloucestershire family, heir to £10,000 a year, who was studying to be ordained not because he had a real calling but because he wanted to be useful. He said he would finish his course because he did not like leaving things halfway, but would then team up with Lloyd-Baker so long as the older man was there to oversee and help him.

The result was the Hardwicke Reformatory, called at first in deference to Brenton 'The Children's Friend School'. It was built on a six-acre patch of uncultivated ground on Lloyd-Baker's estate, between the Severn and the canal, which would make absconding difficult. It was very simply built, a long brick building with a cottage at one end for the bailiff or superintendent, and two rooms at the other for the schoolmaster. For the first two years George Bengough was that schoolmaster. The lack of elaboration was practical and financial, but also because Lloyd-Baker understood only too well the problems of what one might call the 'prodigal son syndrome' – resentment from the deserving that the undeserving are given a better deal. He was in any case a great believer in plain living and hard outdoor work.

> I know of no employment which will allay the excitement and tranquillise the mind so as to prepare it to be acted upon by a firm kindness, like steady digging.[24]

The Reformatory opened in 1852 with three hardened young criminals:

> We got three boys from London of the worst class that we could find who would come voluntarily to us as at that time we had no Law and no Government aid to help us ..... One had been convicted seven times, another nine times and the 3rd was doubtful but it was believed that he had been eleven times convicted.[25]

First results were extremely good. In the first report in 1854 to 'friends and supporters' Lloyd-Baker was able to say:

> It appears then that out of fifty boys who have been under treatment this year, twenty have left the school. Of these four have absconded or turned out ill, and the remaining sixteen i.e. eighty per cent of the whole who have left the school, give hopes, more or less certain, of a confirmed restoration to an honest life.[26]

After the passing of the 1854 Act, the police in Cheltenham were able to co-operate, and concentrated on identifying the ringleaders, effectively disbanding the gangs. In 1863 Lloyd-Baker reported:

> This is what I had always hoped from the beginning .... that Reformatories by stopping contagion, and by breaking up gangs, would do far more to prevent the hitherto innocent from being tempted into crime, than the utmost they could effect in reforming those who had already fallen.[27]

Lloyd-Baker was a man of faith but not of dogma, proud of the fact that he could work equally well with Archbishop Manning, a Roman Catholic, and Mary Carpenter, a Unitarian. Apart from his practical success at Hardwicke, he had enormous influence in organising, encouraging, and bringing to public notice the reformatory movement. Although he objected to the term 'reformed boys' because he said you could never be absolutely sure, and although he did not want a system which tried to work without punishment, he was quite certain where the emphasis should lie if society was to be genuinely improved:

> The main question therefore should be what society should do with its doubtful and corrupt elements before punishment in order to prevent crime, and what after punishment is to become of the discharged? In comparison with that, what happens in prison is, after all, of secondary consideration, though it may be important enough. Let us be satisfied if in the jail we do not corrupt body and soul .... I cannot share the confidence of so many men in chains, bolts, locks, barred windows, cells and party-coloured jackets.[28]

If a reformatory were to live up to its name, therefore, it would be a Hardwicke and not a Parkhurst.

Public anxiety, followed by parliamentary anxiety, concerning the problem of juvenile mendicancy and lawbreaking, increased throughout the 1840s and early 1850s. A report of 1851 spoke of:

> hundreds of poor children in all great towns training up as thieves ..... the children are sent out in the morning with watercress, chalkstones, cocoanut husks etc. and at night with firewood. The whole of these children are dirty, ragged, without covering to head or feet. They must bring home a certain sum or value, whether obtained by begging, selling or stealing ..... Many of the boys are only six or seven years of age.[29]

Another report from Staffordshire noted:

> The practice of sending poor children out to beg prevails most extensively in this district; vast numbers are daily dispatched from the filthy lodging houses, and spread themselves all over the surrounding villages.[30]

Both these reports were quoted by Lord Shaftesbury in 1853, in the course of introducing a bill on child mendicancy in the House of Lords: 'Childhood was the seedtime of crime,' he told his hearers:

> and if they wished to remove children from temptation, they must either abate the noxious influences to which they were exposed, or remove the child from its reach; and it showed very clearly, as he thought, and in the most forcible manner, that if they protected the early years of the child, principle, good sense, experience, and habit would protect him in his maturer life, and that it was but the ill-trained and neglected child that grew into the desperate uncontrollable man.[31]

The chief mover in the House of Commons was Charles Adderley (1814–1905), member for North Staffordshire, who had inherited great estates in North Staffordshire and neighbouring Warwickshire. He was well aware of the problems of fast-growing populations in the Midlands. His estate at Saltley, near Birmingham, which in 1835 supported 400 inhabitants, grew during his lifetime to 27,000. Adderley planned the area's growth as early as 1837, trying to avoid the formation of slums, and it was here, in 1852, that he founded his own reformatory, which opened a few months after Hardwicke. In his speech at the second reading of the bill in the Commons he

> rejoiced that transportation in such cases was now about to cease; but though he rejoiced at that cessation, it must be remembered that, at all events, now, these children, if not otherwise taken care of and reformed within the precincts of this country, would in the end augment the amount of adult crime. Of 28,000 committals in this country in one year, 13,000, or nearly 50 per cent, were of persons under seventeen years of age.[32]

The Times newspaper, which wielded immense influence on public opinion, weighed in on the side of the reformatory movement, provided always that it could be carried out without putting too much weight on the taxpayer. In January 1854 a long leading article appeared, inspired by the recently-published first year's report from the Hardwicke school: 'Some plan or other must be attempted, for what else are we to do with the rising generation of crime?' it thundered in the style which caused Anthony Trollope to nickname it *The Jupiter*.

> Where can we now transport them? What shore will receive them? In what abyss can we stow them away? How shall we insulate them? The earth is saturated with British crime, and refuses to hold more; but at home we are full to overflowing. We must begin at the fountainhead, and if possible, reform them whom we cannot either transport, or shut up, or destroy, or set at large.

It saw, as many people saw, salvation in the mobilising of the middle class on behalf of the lesser mortals of society. 'There is no machinery, no institution, no system like an educated gentleman whose heart is in his work.'[33]

This was the general feeling. The growing Reformatory movement wanted help from the Government in the form of legal backing, and perhaps some finance, but not too much legal backing or too much finance which would inevitably lead to regulation. The general opinion of the workers on the ground is well-expressed in a letter from another young landowner to Thomas Barwick Lloyd-Baker, when the 1854 Act had been in place for a couple of years, and the Government was considering further regulation and a general tidying up of the very disparate results of reformatory establishment:

> I am rather afraid of your grand company but if they will only be content to patronise the workers and leave them alone, that can't do much harm .... You don't want a stiff uniform system, what you do want is a lot of fellows who will work at the thing for the love of it, with their heads and hearts in the right place, under the control of course of Government as far as inspection is concerned, because if they contribute money it is only fair and right to see that it is properly spent, the Inspector might visit monthly or weekly if he liked, but to lay down a set of stereotyped rules and regulations going into details and on an expensive plan would disgust many of the most zealous friends of the movement.

The letter was sent from Bleasdale in Lancashire and signed 'William James Garnett.'[34]

The unease which this letter expresses was caused by the build-up towards a second Act of 1857. On the whole, the first definitive Act, of 1854 met with nothing but approval from the workers on the ground. 'An Act for the better Care and Reformation of Youthful Offenders in Great Britain' contained only eight fairly brief clauses. Reformatories were to be certificated and then subject to inspection by the Inspectors of Prisons. Convicted juveniles under the age of 16 could be sent to a reformatory for any suitable period from two to five years. Importantly, such offenders had first to serve a prison sentence of at least two weeks, and if they absconded they might be punished by a gaol term of up to three months. The Treasury was to be liable for the 'Cost of Care and Maintenance' of the child, or such part of it as could not be recovered from the parents, and a good part of the short Act dealt with the knotty problem of how to compel parents to subsidise their children's detention. The most notable omission was that of any reference to building and staffing – this was left to voluntary enterprise.

The Act passed on 14 July 1854 with very little fanfare. Only 92 members voted and they passed it 69 to 23. The clause putting inspection into the hands of the Prison Inspectors was short-lived. In 1856 the Reverend Sydney Turner was appointed Inspector for Reformatories, and the rapidly-growing number of reformatories ensured a minimal time for inspecting each one. One day, or even half a day, a year was the normal rate – light enough, one would think, to reassure even William James Garnett – though in fact he managed to have some lengthy argumentative spats with Sydney Turner over the running of his own reformatory at Bleasdale.

Once the 1854 Act had been passed, the trickle of foundations became almost a flood. Three years later, by July 1857, 36 reformatories had been certificated, and the ambition of the enthusiasts was that every county should have at least one.

Notes

[1]   King, P., 'The Rise of Juvenile Delinquency, 1780–1841', *Past and Present* (August 1998), 116.

[2]   Ibid, 117.

[3]   Carpenter, M., *Reformatory Schools for the Children of the Perishing and Dangerous Classes* (1851), 211.

[4]   Ibid, 288.

[5]   Quoted in Rev. W.L. Clay, *The Prison Chaplain* (1861), 464.

[6]   Carpenter, *Reformatory Schools*, 263.

[7]   *Dictionary of National Biography* (OUP, 1975), 1172.

[8]   Carpenter, *Reformatory Schools*, Preface.

[9]   Ibid, 2.

[10]   Ibid, 121.

[11]   Ibid, 147.

[12]   Ibid, 156.

[13]   Ibid, 176.

[14]   Ibid, 226.

[15]   The Royal Philanthropic Society, *The Story of the School 1788–1953* (1954).

[16]   Turner, S., *Annual Report to the Philanthropic Society* (1846).

[17]   *Illustrated London News*, 13 March 1847.

[18]   Carpenter, *Reformatory Schools*, 321.

[19]   *Victoria County History of Gloucestershire*, Vol II (1907), 177.

[20]   Duckworth, J.S., *The Hardwicke Reformatory School* (Bristol and Gloucestershire Archaeological Society, 1995), 163.

[21]   Lloyd-Baker, T.B., unpublished Autobiography, GA, D3549/25/7/4.

[22]   Brenton, E. Letter to T.B. Lloyd-Baker, GA, D3549/25/2/1.

[23]   Lloyd-Baker, Autobiography.

[24]   Lloyd-Baker, T.B., Paper read to the British Association, 1854. Quoted in his Autobiography.

[25]   Lloyd-Baker, Autobiography.

[26]   Report on Hardwicke, 1854. GA, D3549/23/2/3.

[27]   Ibid.

[28]   Quoted in Professor von Holtzenddorff, *An English Country Squire, as sketched at Hardwicke Court* (1878).

[29]   *Hansard*, 5 July 1853. Letter quoted by Lord Shaftesbury to the House of Lords in his speech to the House of Lords on 'Juvenile Mendicancy.'

[30]   *Hansard*, 5 July 1853. Rev. John Clay *Annual Report* to Preston Magistrates, 1851. Quoted by Lord Shaftesbury in his speech to the House of Lords.

[31]   *Hansard*, 5 July 1853. Speech by Lord Shaftesbury to the House of Lords.

[32]   *Hansard*, 1 August 1853. Charles Adderley in the House of Commons.

[33]   *The Times*, 3 Jan. 1854.

[34]   WJ Garnett Letter to Lloyd-Baker, 26 Feb. 1856. GA, D3549/25/3/11.

CHAPTER TWO

The Reformatory Movement in Lancashire

The huge growth of urban populations with all its attendant problems, including a high rate of crime, was nowhere felt more acutely, or for longer, than in Lancashire, a situation which found its analyst and its most vivid portrayer in Friedrich Engels. *The Condition of the Working Class in England* is a young man's book (Engels was in his early 20s when he spent two years, 1842–4, in Manchester), and the enthusiasm, the indignation, and the exaggerations are those of a young man. However, it still gives the best first-hand picture of the worst side of the industrial revolution, and leaves the modern reader in no doubt at all as to how and why juvenile destitution and crime flourished in this period.

By the 1841 census Manchester and Liverpool, the largest centres of population in Lancashire, were each approaching a population of

2: London Slums. 'Over London by Rail', Gustav Doré.

250,000 – a more than three-fold increase since 1801. There were many industrial reasons for this explosion, though Engels emphasised cotton, the area he knew best from working within it, which 'has thoroughly revolutionised this county, converting it from an obscure, ill-cultivated swamp into a lively, busy region, multiplying its population tenfold in eighty years' causing not only Liverpool and Manchester, but Bolton, Rochdale, Oldham, Preston, Ashton, Stalybridge, 'and a whole list of other manufacturing towns to spring up as if by a magic touch.'[1]

But this massive increase in output was accompanied by terrible effects upon those squeezed relentlessly to the bottom of the social pile. Engels was in no doubt as to where the blame lay – squarely at the door of the middle classes, the 'bourgeoisie', whose attitude he summed up in the anecdote of the acquaintance with whom he walked in Manchester:

> and spoke to him of the bad, unwholesome method of building, the frightful condition of the working people's quarters, and assserted that I had never seen so ill-built a city. The man listened quietly to the end, and said at the corner where we parted "And yet there is a great deal of money made here; good morning sir". It is utterly indifferent to the English bourgeois whether his working men starve or not, if only he makes money.[2]

Engels was not the only one to express this point of view. It was said of the Reverend John Clay (1796–1858), chaplain to the Preston House of Correction, and a notable influence on new initiatives in the treatment of crime and criminals:

> He was one of the first to preach the doctrine, common enough now, that the heartless selfishness of the upper classes, the disgraceful ignorance of, and indifference to, the brutal degradation in which they suffer the poor to lie, is the primary cause of almost all the crime in the country.[3]

In his description of the unacceptable face of Manchester prosperity, Engels pointed out that the layout of the town, and the segregation of its various components, ensured that 'a person may live in it for years, and go in and out daily, without coming into contact with a working-people's quarter or even with workers'[4] whose rookeries lay behind the main thoroughfares. Two of these daily middle-class commuters whom Engels castigated as unthinking and uncaring in their pursuit of wealth, were the brothers Robert (1780–1852) and William (1782–1863) Garnett, who came in daily from their smart houses in Cheetham and Lark Hill, Salford, to their office in Pall Mall, where they traded as cotton and fustian dealers. When William unsuccessfully stood for the Conservative interest in Salford in 1832, his election manifesto was directed almost totally at the commercial interests of his townsmen – Free Trade, the Corn Laws, the

The Rev.ᵈ John Clay, B.D.

3: Rev. John Clay. Reproduced with the kind permission of the depositor and the County Archivist, Lancashire Record Office.

East India Company's monopoly, taxes, the situation in Ireland, tithes, and the necessity to cut government expenditure. He expressed an opinion that 'the existence of slavery in our West Indian Colonies must be a source of regret to every humane mind', but said nothing about the possibility of ameliorating the situation of English workers.[5]

Engels knew what he was talking about, because on the one hand as a young man working in the office of his father's cotton-thread business he had the entrée to this middle-class society, and on the other, it was the working-class world which his reading and philosophy led him to explore – an exploration which was greatly facilitated by Mary Burns, an illiterate working girl with whom he lived.

His descriptions of the worst of Manchester slums are famous, and although it is true to say that in 1842 the situation was exacerbated by a severe slump in the cotton trade, these slumps were cyclical, returning with depressing regularity about every six years. In 1836, it was estimated that 50,000 cotton operatives out of a work force of 80,000 were on short time.[6] Moreover, the new industrial world depended on a pool of unemployed labour, what to Malthus was the 'surplus population' and which General Booth later came to christen 'the submerged tenth.' Nonetheless, there was a great deal of serious thinking, both local and national, about the problems and the possible means for their amelioration, activity which the hot-headed Engels tended to dismiss as pure hypocrisy.

If Lancashire had some of the most pressing problems, it also produced some varied answers. 'It must be confessed that act-of-parliament philanthropy is no match for volunteer benevolence'[7] is a statement which sums up a strong strand in the thinking of the time. In the matter of juvenile delinquency the initial reliance on 'volunteer benevolence' produced a spectrum of experimental response out of which was finally distilled a national pattern which would have been less rich, and probably less successful, if it had not grown from so many different starting points.

The Reverend John Clay (1796–1858), quoted above and previously mentioned, was a very influential figure, though he had no direct connection with the foundation of any particular reformatory. In 1823 he took the post of chaplain at Preston House of Correction, just after the Gaol Act had tidied up a sprawling situation with regard to crime and punishment. It practically abolished the death penalty for any crime short of murder, and laid down new guidelines for the better regulation of prisons, including the appointment of chaplains with responsibility not only for the souls of prisoners, but also as far as possible for their education.

A fairly enlightened magistracy paid Clay a salary of £250 to ensure he would undertake no other duties, and for the next 35 years he laboured in a post which offered rewards but could also be deeply depressing. His annual reports, at first covering a modest handwritten ten pages, enlarged over the years to 50 or 60 printed pages, documents full – perhaps too full – of statistics concerning everything to do with crime and criminals in society. He provided tables showing Lancashire crime statistics compared with those in all other counties; incidence of crime committed by those born locally compared with those born elsewhere (mostly Irish); tables showing types of offence, number of committals, number of recommittals, proportions of criminals to population, actual crime, detected crime, juvenile crime. He accompanied these with an ever-growing number of personal histories which prisoners wrote for him, or dictated if they were unable to write; giving an unparalleled insight into the seamier side of life in the urban centres of Lancashire. These reports were widely circulated and Clay, who also became well known for his involvement in housing and sanitation issues, was increasingly called upon as an adviser to politicians and a witness before committees.

Reforming criminals of all ages was an idea whose time had come. The new prisons, of which Pentonville (1842) was the first, were dedicated to the idea that reform was possible. Inevitably there was a backlash, most trenchantly expressed by Thomas Carlyle in his article on 'Model Prisons', a diatribe which was perhaps too violent to be as damaging as it might have been.

> Howard abated gaol-fever, but it seems to me he has been the innocent cause of a far more distressing fever which rages high just now ..... that tumultuous frothing ocean-tide of benevolent sentimentality, 'abolition of punishment', all absorbing 'prison-discipline', and general morbid sympathy, instead of hearty hatred for scoundrels.[8]

The principle of the new prisons was segregation and as with all good ideas it took a wrong turning in the hands of those who carried it to

4: Preston House of Correction. Reproduced by permission of Lancashire County Library and Information Service. http://lanternimages.lancashire.gov.uk / No. 639.

excess – at one time Pentonville prisoners were hooded to prevent them recognizing each other, a system which signally failed to work. Prisoners in isolation with almost nothing to do (the greater number were illiterate so that the issue of Bibles was of little value) had more time to think of ways of circumventing the rules than the prison staff had to think of ways of preventing them. Moreover it became apparent that there was a real danger of mental illness in an existence so desperately circumscribed.

John Clay became convinced of the value of segregation, although his ideas were modified by long experience and a real personal interest in the prisoners who came within his orbit. 'Contamination, if the system be perfectly administered, is impossible,' but of course it was not possible unless the jails could be rebuilt. He was too honest not to state the objections including 'the tendency to insanity which it is said to produce in prisoners who undergo a long confinement' although that problem, under his system of constant personal visiting of the men in their cells, and the sensible deployment of work and education, had not shown itself in Preston. The system did not work everywhere. In Glasgow for instance, where the scheme had been fully tried, 'the recommitals are 50 per cent.'[9]

Although at first Clay had found a good deal of opposition to his theories from some of his magistrates, gradually he won them over, and from the 1840s onwards was given almost carte blanche in organising the methods of the Preston House of Correction, so far as the available buildings, finances and staffing would allow. But it was the personal element which counted. There was nothing perfunctory about his chapel services or his treatment of individual prisoners, and even remembering that his biography was written by a devoted son within three years of the father's death, it is still possible to draw the conclusion that here was a very remarkable man who by working strictly according to his Christian principles was able to have a great and spreading influence on the whole business of prisons and prisoners.

Clay's work with the prisoners under his care depended on providing them with opportunities for education, and (to him much more important) persuading them to accept religion into their lives. At this distance it is very difficult to decide how far he was successful in this. From the beginning he had nothing but praise for the decorum with which even hardened criminals attended his services, which he geared with infinite pains to their understanding. He was well aware of the problem of hypocrisy – prisoners pretending conversion to make their lives easier – but reading between the lines of his copious reports it is possible to assume that many prisoners co-operated because they had a real respect for the man he was, and genuinely wanted to give him satisfaction. His chief influence clearly was his unfeigned interest in them as human beings, however depraved, whose lives could be turned round. They recognised his honesty and his kindness as he went outside his brief to write their letters, visit their homes, and argue on their behalf with the authorities about basic necessities like clean towels and fresh water. He was able to report that only twice in 35 years was he 'insulted' by a prisoner.

Literature on the American system of segregation greatly influenced Clay (although the American system in many cases was exaggerated into considerable cruelty). He persuaded the governor and magistrates to adapt part of the House of Correction into single cells where prisoners could be separated. The building was not easy to adapt, and it was never done very thoroughly, but he felt that the experience was often a pivotal one. In particular, Clay felt that this system was absolutely necessary to break the chain of evil influence of the hardened criminals on the young: 'The child of 14, or 10, or even 8 years is now turned into a yard or day-room tenanted by 40 or 50 old criminals.'[10]

> I have seen children who upon the first day of their imprisonment were crying with shame and apprehension, become in "a little week" careless and indifferent, reckless and turbulent, and I have seen, in too many instances, such children committed again and again upon charges of felony, and eventually sentenced to transportation.[11]

The plight of the young offender became more and more important in Clay's eyes. 'What is to become of these unfortunate creatures? Some with no homes – some with worse than none – without employment – without character – destitute and demoralized.'[12] In the 1840s his thinking went no further than the idea of a 'well-organised House of Refuge for the reception of young and desperate criminals on their discharge from prison.'[13] However, over the years, under the influence of Mary Carpenter and others, his mind turned to reformatory schools. Once the 1854 Act was passed, he had no doubt of their value. His report published in 1855 argued the need for a north Lancashire reformatory which could deal with cases in that area. Clay felt real concern for the 'neglected and much to be pitied creatures' returned after their seven or 14 days' incarceration to their homes:

> What homes? homes of vice and brutality! Homes in unused outbuildings, stables, privies, or other similar shelters, in which orphans or children "turned out of doors" are accustomed to pass their nights.[14]

The mindset of the time prevented his coming, at least in public, to the logical conclusion that many such children had to steal in order to live, and his plea for 'corrective treatment' rather than the jail's revolving door was backed, as perhaps it would have to be at any period, by the argument of value for money. 'The child will cost much less by a few years' proper training, than he would by a few years of alternate imprisonment and crime.'[15]

In October 1853 a group of Manchester business men met to consider the setting up of a 'Ragged and Industrial School', which later developed into a reformatory. Manchester had had one Ragged School since 1847. This would be the second, and was to serve the inaccurately named district of 'Angel Meadow' which was as poor a ghetto as any in the town.

Out of this meeting came the 'Angel Meadow District Ragged and Industrial School', later to be reconstructed as 'The Manchester and Salford Reformatory for Juvenile Criminals.'[16] The school opened in the autumn of 1854, closely monitored by a hard-working committee of nine gentlemen who met once a week to direct everything except the actual contact with the children. The published rules were:

1. School to open and close with prayer.
2. Instruction in the holy scriptures daily.
3. Both education and industrial work to be provided.
4. The children must be from the lowest class of vagrants or beggars.
5. School to be open from 7 a.m. to 4 p.m.
6. The subcommittee to sanction all expenditure.
7. The greatest economy consistent with good health to be used in the diet.

Although the school opened after the Act, this was not a reformatory, but was still run on the voluntary principle, entirely supported by voluntary contributions. The managers soon found that they could not in conscience take in children until four p.m. and then turn them out on the streets until seven next morning. The first important change was that beds were provided for ten children, and then a further ten. But the premises were poor and the money slow to dribble in. Within the year, in October 1855, the school was hit by a typhoid epidemic which killed the schoolmaster. The building was closed as unfit, and the 13 boarding children removed to the workhouse.

This bad start inspired some new thinking, as did the fact that a local lady, a Miss Pearce, had left £1,000 in her will to any local body which would open a reformatory. It was found that most of the children who attended, although on a voluntary basis, had been convicted at some time, so that the idea of a reformatory took root in the committee's mind. At some stage, as with other similar establishments, they realised that it was not practicable to combine convicted youngsters from the courts with a voluntary sector. The committee bought eight acres of land at Blackley, on the northern edge of Manchester, and built a reformatory, which opened as such and was certificated in October 1857.

There was a strict and rigorous timetable of industrial work, education, prayer and domestic tasks, supported by a limited, monotonous and (in terms of quantity) inadequate diet. The dietary was passed by the inspectors in October 1857 when the Reformatory received its certificate, but a month later the boys complained, and the bread allowance was raised, though only for those working outdoors. It was necessary to run these early reformatories with the most stringent economy, and there was always the powerful argument that the public must not be antagonised, nor the criminal classes encouraged, by the belief that life was better on the inside. However the suspicion remains that, whether they admitted it to themselves or not, it was to the institution's advantage to deal with inmates whose energy levels were kept low. Indeed, given the very small number of staff expected to run such a place, this was a necessity.

The philanthropists of Liverpool, the great seaport, tackled their problem in a different way from Manchester cottonopolis. In January 1855 a very large body of the influential members of Liverpool society was called together 'for the purpose of considering such measures as might be deemed necessary for the establishment of a Reformatory Institution in Liverpool.' The working sub-committee was very much smaller, and took its responsibilities very seriously, meeting every week.[17]

The result was the establishment of the training ship *Akbar*, using an old ship donated by the Lords of the Admiralty, which cost nearly £2,000 to get into some sort of habitable order and even so lasted less than ten years before it had to be replaced. All the boys trained on the *Akbar* were destined for the merchant navy, so, at the same time, the committee began to look for a site where they might establish a land-based school for children who were not physically able to undergo the rigours of a naval training and could not be expected to make their living at sea. This part of the plan, as well as the setting up of a girls' reformatory, were delayed until the *Akbar* was running satisfactorily. The Girls' Reformatory at Mount Vernon opened in 1857, the Liverpool Farm School at Newton-le-Willows in 1858.

The 41 rules which were discussed and passed in November 1855 by the committee with the help of the Inspector of Prisons have not survived. However, they were demanding on both the boys and the staff. The staff's uniforms were as strictly directed as the boys' clothing, and they were to live on the same rations. This also applied to the superintendent, who was appointed at the meagre salary of £80 a year, but allowed to bring his wife and child with him to live on board.

The *Akbar* took in its first boys in February 1856: nine of them, three from Liverpool, and six of Lloyd-Baker's 'trained boys' from Hardwicke 'to set the tone.' These were exchanged for four Liverpool boys. Immediately the committee were almost overwhelmed by suggestions for committals and exchanges with other reformatories. Only a month after opening they had nearly 30 boys on board and called a halt 'until the regulations and discipline on board are more systematized.'

At least one other very short-lived reformatory was set up in Liverpool. George Melly, a wealthy young man in his early 20s with a social conscience, opened the Mason Street Reformatory in 1856. As his own address was Mason Street it would appear that he used part of his own property, but little information remains. What there is is contained in two reports to his supporters, in 1856 and 1857, the second of which announced his intention of closing down at the end of the year, having had 33 boys in all on the premises, most of them for very short periods. In his report, Melly attributed the early closure of his experiment to the fact that:

> We are not prepared to bear the weight and responsibility of a Reformatory Prison certified under the Act; we think that, while private generosity and exertion should ever pioneer the way in new works of charity and social improvement, large schemes (like the reformation of juvenile offenders) when proved to be sound, should be carried out at the expense of the whole community which they benefit.

In fact, having started with high hopes, Melly had clearly become disillusioned. Boys, who were required to undertake to stay a year, left within a matter of weeks, not relishing the discipline, and, far from being properly co-operative and grateful for what was done for them, 'the fixed impression in their minds [is] that they are conferring an inestimable favour upon the Managers by consenting to remain in the house at all.'[18]

By 1858 there were embryonic reformatories in most English counties and Sydney Turner in his report of that year, summarised his general philosophy of the movement:

> First of all their tone of discipline, dietary, industrial occupation, lodging, habits of recreation, etc. etc. must be made strict, and must have something of the hardness which St. Paul prescribes as an essential element of the Christian training and which, if needful for the formation and development of characters of the common class, must *a fortiori* be still more wanting for the correction and reformation of those who have fallen away in weakness and been corrupted by vice. Self will, disorder, idleness and sensual indulgence have been more or less the causes of their perversion. A manly training to obedience, regularity, industry and self-control is the needful remedy. Confidence without familiarity on the part of the child, kindness without weakness or flattery on the part of the teacher; earnestness in everything – work, devotion, school instruction or play; self-respect in personal cleanliness and neatness; order in daily habits and meals; these are the marks of a successful reformatory.[19]

Thomas Arnold of Rugby might have altered the emphasis a little, but one feels he would in general have subscribed to this as his blueprint for a good public school.

The reformatories were private institutions, and although they mainly agreed in principle, their methods varied considerably. *Akbar* discipline was always and necessarily severe, but at times it was positively savage. The boys were not only confined in space (Captain Fenwick's request for a playground on shore was shelved for many years), they were also being trained in highly dangerous physical circumstances. It was felt to be appropriate to feed them on the salt beef, soup and biscuit of the merchant navy, in spite of protests from the inspectorate. Boys were sometimes punished en masse by being kept standing to attention on deck for two or even three hours at a stretch, and the cells, without light and to which boys were sentenced on a diet of bread and water, were used long after they had become illegal. The death toll was far higher than in the shore-based reformatories, a fact which the inspectors accepted with remarkable equanimity, commenting on it occasionally as an unavoidable fact of shipboard life.

Still, *Akbar* caught the public imagination most successfully. No dignitary visiting Liverpool, from the Duke of Clarence downwards, seems to have left without an obligatory visit to the training ships. The cleanliness which is next to godliness was never more apparent to the visitor than on a ship under naval discipline, and the boys' timed and co-ordinated exercises in the rigging were far more impressive, and easier to interpret as successful reformation, than the sight of boys digging endless rows of potatoes in the shore-based establishments.

The Reverend John Clay at Preston was not satisfied with the establishment of a reformatory in Manchester and one in Liverpool, necessary though they both were. He had set his heart on a third one to serve the area in which he was personally interested, north Lancashire.

'I am doing my poor best towards the establishment of a Reformatory School for North Lancashire' he wrote to Mary Carpenter in November 1855.[20] 'The press is on our side and we have many well-wishers among the justices but ..... I much fear that we shall be able to do little or nothing in the matter, for we have no Mr Sturges, or Mr Baker, or Mr Bengough, or Miss Carpenter, who will give time and energies to the matter.' However, although no document showing a direct connection has been found between John Clay and the foundation of the reformatory he longed to see, his efforts were more successful than perhaps he knew. Considering the great influence his prison reports had on all interested parties who read them, it is not surprising to find that soon after the above letter was written, activity began to stir in north Lancashire, as he had hoped. By December 1856, he was able to report:

> You will be glad to learn that our North Lancashire Reformatory is rising from the ground as rapidly as possible. The originator of it, Mr Garnett, is a first-class man both morally and intellectually, and under his influence, and by God's blessing, it cannot but prosper.[21]

It was sad that John Clay himself did not long survive the opening of the reformatory he had wished for, and although he was involved in conversations at the planning stage, it seems unlikely that he saw it on the ground. His health had been deteriorating for some years, and he had longed for someone to offer him a quiet parish in the country, but it did not happen. He wrote his last report for the Preston magistrates in the summer of 1858, then resigned, and died soon after.

Notes

[1]   Engels, F., *The Condition of the Working Class in England* (1845, 1st English Edition 1892. OUP reprint 1999), 21.

[2]   Ibid., 282.

[3]   Clay, Rev. W.L., *The Prison Chaplain* (1861), 212.

[4]   Engels, *The Condition*, 58.

[5]   LRO, DDQ/6/20/1.

[6]   Briggs, A., *Victorian Cities* (1963), 134.

[7]   Clay, *Prison Chaplain*, 585.

[8]   Carlyle, T., *Model Prisons* (Latter Day Pamphlets, 1850).

[9]   Clay, J.C., *Report to Visiting Magistrates*, 1838, LRO, QGR 2/37.

[10]   Clay, J.C., *Report*, 1840, LRO, QGR 2/31.

[11]   Clay, J.C., *Report*, 1837, LRO, QGR 2/36.

12   Clay, J.C., *Report*, 1840, LRO, QGR 2/31.

13   Clay, J.C., Ibid.

14   Clay, J.C., *Report*, 1855, LRO, QGR 2/42.

15   Ibid.

16   Information concerning the Manchester and Salford Reformatory from the Governor's Journal, LRO, DDX 1791/5/2.

17   Information concerning the setting up of the *Akbar* from the Liverpool Juvenile Reformatory Association Minutes, 1855–1863. LRO, DDX 824/1/1.

18   Reports on Mason Street Reformatory School for Juvenile Male Delinquents 1856–1857 in George Melly, Stray Leaves, 1856–94, Volume I. Liverpool Record Office and Local History Service, H 825 MEL.

19   Inspector of Reformatory Schools of Great Britain, *Report* (1858), Introduction, 15.

20   Clay, W.L., *Prison Chaplain*, Letter quoted, p. 620.

21   Ibid, 621.

CHAPTER THREE

William James Garnett and the founding of Bleasdale

In a number of ways, the Garnett family was typical of its time and place and background. From an undistinguished yeoman holding in the fells above Kirkby Lonsdale, in the first half of the eighteenth century they migrated to Liverpool, enticed, like so many others, by the West Indian trade. In the 1780s John Garnett, with whom we are concerned, briefly joined his brother James in the slave trade, having a part-share in a slaving vessel called the *Garnett*. However, he thought better of this and relocated to Manchester where he prospered as a cotton merchant, though still with interests in Jamaica. After his death his two younger sons, Robert and William, although both were under 20 years of age when their father died, took over the trade with a mixture of flair, determination and hard work.

Both made large fortunes and, by the 1830s, were ready to retire, sell up their handsome Manchester homes and invest in gentrification. Robert's new estate was in Wyresdale, William's in Bleasdale, where, while still living in Salford, he had already built himself a shooting lodge. Later, he moved further up-market to Quernmore Park, near Lancaster. In his declining years, although he occupied himself to a certain extent with country matters, William's real interest was the rapidly-growing web of railways. He was a founder director of the Liverpool and Manchester, and later of the various parts of what is now the West Coast line. His speculations were sometimes more daring than was wise, and in his declining years, when he suffered from Alzheimer's or something similar, the family fortune had begun to spring some quite serious leaks.

William's marriage had been sadly short-lived, his wife dying of consumption in 1821 at the age of 30. The only son to survive childhood, William James, was born less than three years before his mother's death and undoubtedly inherited from her the seeds of the disease against which he struggled for most of his life, and which killed him at the age of 55.

William James can never have been a light-hearted boy, and grew up with a powerful sense of the responsibility of wealth, and an equally powerful sense of religion, which as he grew older hardened into a

5: Bleasdale Tower in 1845 (private collection).

conviction that God's immutable will was discoverable through prayer, and once discovered admitted of no human argument. But he was no hypocrite, and this meant that people divided into those who were immensely impressed by his honesty and undoubted qualities of leadership, and those who were frustrated by his pig-headedness.

At the age of 12 he was sent to school at Rugby, where Thomas Arnold was the newly-appointed headmaster, but whether that great man had any lasting effect on young Garnett's attitude to life it is not possible to say. In fact, he did not stay long, the Warwickshire climate having a bad effect on his weak chest. He was sent instead to Switzerland, and came back aged 16 to Eton. The next step was to Christ Church, Oxford, where he came under the influence of Newman and the Oxford movement. In 1845, the year that Newman 'went to Rome', William James also felt called to become Roman Catholic, but changed his mind when his father threatened to throw him out of the house. It is easy to be cynical about such changes of mind, but there is no doubt that although William James hardly ever referred to his father in his diaries except rather formally as 'Mr W.G', the two were immensely important to each other. The wife and mother had died, and so had two little brothers. His sister was married and fully occupied with her family in London. William James' God did not demand that he break up his father's life and his own, and he remained for the rest of his life a loyal though not

5: Bleasdale Terrain.
Photograph by
Angus Winchester,
2007.

uncritical member of the Church of England. In 1846 he married, and
after a comprehensive wedding tour on the continent, lasting eight
months, the young couple settled down at Bleasdale Tower, the elder
William having by this time moved to Quernmore Park.

At this period the eastern half of Bleasdale was a wild unenclosed part
of the old Forest of Lancaster. It is still one of the remoter parts of north
Lancashire, five miles from Chipping on the one side, and seven miles
from Garstang on the other, facing the high bleak moors. When the
Garnetts first took up residence at Bleasdale Tower it was indeed remote.
Thus, it proved extremely difficult to persuade any clergyman to settle
there to serve the little church at Admarsh which the family were
instrumental in rebuilding in 1835. But for people with money it was not
so bad, for they had their horses, their vehicles, and their servants. As a
young man William James increasingly used the house for weekends,
often walking up from the new railway station at Garstang and leaving
his luggage to be picked up later. It was here that he developed, like many
men of his time and class, a great interest in agricultural improvement.
The naked moors of the Bleasdale estate, with some dozen rough little
farms, were a prime ground for experiment. In the ten years after his
marriage William James developed this interest, always keeping one,
sometimes two, of the farms in his own hands and experimenting largely
in drainage, suitable crops and stock improvement. In 1849 he wrote a
prize essay on 'Farming in Lancashire' for the Royal Agricultural Society.
The only restraint was that, although effectively a landowner, he was not

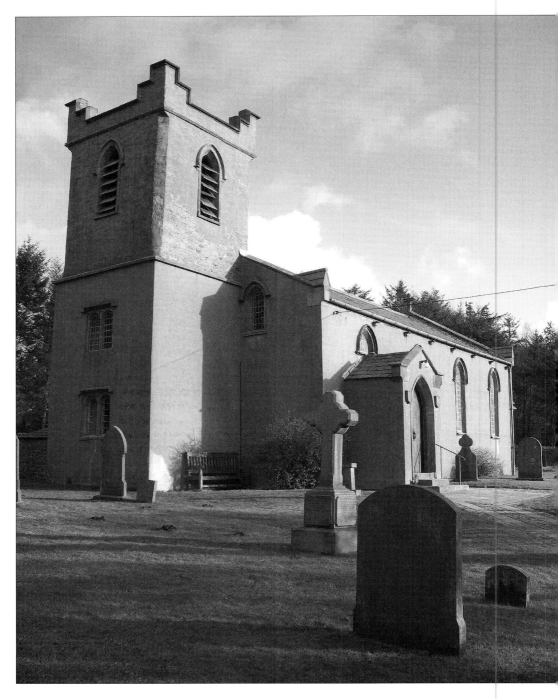

7: Admarsh Church.
Photograph by Angus
Winchester, 2008.

independent. To the end of his life his father held the purse-strings: in January 1853 William James' diary records: 'Engaged with my father for some little time discussing Bleasdale expenses. Rather a warm altercation especially respecting Brook Barns.'[1]

The younger Garnett quickly settled into his place as a country gentleman. He qualified as a magistrate soon after his marriage and attended Petty Sessions and the Board of Guardians very much more responsibly than many others. In those days attendance was voluntary, and he was not infrequently one of only two magistrates to turn up – occasionally the only one. William James worked his stint as visiting magistrate to the Preston House of Correction, and became acquainted with John Clay. There are numerous diary references to their meetings in Preston, and Clay, as is clear from his letter to Mary Carpenter previously quoted, thought him an entirely suitable person to undertake the responsibility of providing a reformatory for north Lancashire.

Garnett's interest in various forms of education had been apparent for some time and continued after the foundation of the reformatory. He was responsible for building new schools at Bleasdale, as well as Calder Vale and Quernmore. He was an early, though not a foundation, member of the board at Rossall school. He had known Nathaniel Woodard for a number of years, met him in London and Brighton, talked education, and visited his foundation at Hurstpierpoint: 'saw all the establishment which is very interesting and very extraordinary.'[2] However, until 1856 his very factual diaries convince that his chief interest was agriculture and the improvement of his land – attending stock sales, frequently with Thomas Cranston, his father's knowledgeable and efficient land agent, visiting experimental farms, visiting family and friends, and entertaining them at Bleasdale.

Although William James' diaries rarely record his thinking, reading them gives the impression of a driven man, searching for the activity which would justify him to himself and, more importantly, to that watchful and demanding God. He may have been pursued by the knowledge that his health would never be good and he must make the most of his time. Once, in an uncharacteristic entry, he suddenly commented 'I am almost tired of shooting, it is such a waste of time and so cruel, that I begin to think it demoralizing and destructive of true religious habits and feelings; I must give it up.'[3] But he didn't, or at least not then, although he did so later in his life.

This relentless search for the right way to use oneself and one's prosperity undoubtedly led him to embark on far too much, to respond to too many demands, while his character did not permit him to skimp on any of them. As has already been said, the very factual form of his diaries does not allow the reader to follow his thinking in any detail, but conclusions can be drawn from the frequency with which certain activities are mentioned, and the amount of time and attention given up to them. He seems to have succumbed suddenly and completely to the intense interest in reformatory education which was sweeping through certain levels of society in the early 1850s. 'Reformatory mania' is hardly too strong a phrase. At the end of 1855, this intense interest appears, like a light switched on. It was not a gradual conversion.

The first letter from Lloyd-Baker of Hardwicke on 29 December 1855 is clearly an answer to one from someone who has written out of the blue. Lloyd-Baker responded in his typically hearty manner, inviting Garnett to stay with him in January 1856, and meet George Latham manager of the Cheshire Reformatory School. 'I consider Wheatley (W. York) Latham (Cheshire) and Castleman (Hants) to be the three men whom you beginners must look to as examples.'[4] In a second letter, undated but closely following the first, Lloyd-Baker listed the reform-

8: William James Garnett. Reproduced by permission of Lancashire County Library and Information Service.

atories already up and running: Mirfield, Bradwell Hall at Sandbach, Eling in Hampshire, Shinfield near Reading, Peckleton, Saltley near Birmingham, Stony Stratford and Newcastle. As far as can be discovered, not all of these were institutions which survived for a long period, but it is illuminating to note the sudden wave of enthusiasm which led to so many experiments being undertaken as soon as the 1854 Act gave the go-ahead.

It is quite difficult for the modern reader to accept as sufficiently serious the commitment of someone like Lloyd-Baker who responded with extra enthusiasm to Garnett's first letter because it identified them both as Etonians, and who arranged his first visit having regard to the fact that: 'The last week in Jan. – 21 to 26 – I'm booked to get a little hunting at Cheltenham,' and who introduced Charles Castleman, principal manager of the school at Eling in Hampshire as: 'worth anything. You may find him often in town at the Union Club – Trafalgar Square.'[5] However, this disbelief has to be suspended. Although it is possible to smile in passing, full respect has to be paid to a man of Lloyd-Baker's integrity and wisdom.

Garnett accepted the invitation and a hand-written notebook shows how keen he was to benefit from others' experience. The early pages read like a direct transcript from Lloyd-Baker's conversation:

> The chief part of the Boys' education must be <u>physical</u> not so much <u>intellectual</u> except in so far as the latter can assist in applying the former to the best advantage; they have their living to get when they quit the school as <u>labourers</u> not as schoolmasters ....
>
> There must be no risk of divided authority on the premises, and attendant evils; the best locality a retired place where not liable to intrusion from strangers and the boys to be made <u>lions</u> of by smart people ....
>
> Twentyfive or thirty Boys in an establishment are quite sufficient, and if more required another house must be provided. The 'family' system of Mettray nothing more nor less than that which prevails in our own English public schools, Eton etc. of different tutors' and dames' Houses, where the boys are boarded, only it is developed further with an especial object; there is no other way of managing a large number of boys or men; what would the Colonel of a Regiment do without his Captains of companies ......
>
> Most desirable at first, if possible, to get a man as superintendent who has been trained to a certain extent in an existing reformatory, and who could bring with him a few boys, 4 5 or 6 whom he knows well and who have made some little progress in their Reformation, these would form a nucleus of good conduct and better feeling, with which to work upon any newcomers, otherwise to start at once with new man and fresh boys would involve great risk of disappointment and failure for some little time.[6]

Garnett acquired a reading list and the names and addresses of useful contacts. He learnt all he could on the ground, with another visitor:

> Up to the Reformatory with Mr Latham (Cheshire). I saw the boys at work draining and overlooker or Bailiff at work in the drain cutting the last footing 4ft. deep in clay. I saw pigs and cows (all not quite neat enough for me) a place for boys to wash in a morning. The boys going to dinner at 1, good beef, parsnips and suet pudding, cut up by the Bailiff, the schoolmaster having rung the bell, said grace all standing, one boy acting as cook who has a particular taste for it. Kitchen adjoining with a buttery hatch in the wall.[7]

There are detailed notes on the layout of the very simple buildings at Hardwicke, and more on the kind of tips which one professional can always pick up usefully from another:

Cupboard of medecines in case of illness; some boys will feign this, a dose of salts, lie in bed and no dinner a good remedy for this …. It is desirable for them to have money, because they can buy something with it, and some have had tame rabbits, all this gives them something to stay for, if they thought of running away.[8]

Garnett's notebook contains newspaper cuttings, many of them deriving from Lloyd-Baker, whose greater practical experience and down-to-earth philosophy made him the natural leader of the whole movement. A letter of his in the *Leeds Mercury* as early as November 1854 is typical both of his thinking and his unvarnished style:

A prison is a place for mere punishment; and punishment can but be, and ought to be, inflicted <u>by law</u> and according to a <u>fixed system</u>. But to reform, you require not a <u>system</u> but a <u>man</u>. Such a man as M. Demetz at Mettray or as Mr Sydney Turner at Redhill.[9]

From Hardwicke, Garnett visited Miss Carpenter's Reformatory for Girls at Bristol and the reformatory at Bramford Speke near Exeter. This had been founded the year before on the Hardwicke model and Sir Stafford Northcote, an Eton contemporary, was the manager. Returning by Birmingham, he visited Saltley reformatory and a large industrial school in the town. During the next week he went to Mirfield to see Wheatley Balme's reformatory there. Here he noted:

Discipline more strict in this school than in others I have seen and quite justified by the acuteness of the boys they would (I was told) have a contempt for a milk and water system and would rather be punished in accordance with strict Rules, than that any breach of these would be overlooked – the great object to get them to think they are punished for their good.[10]

There were as yet only eight boys in this reformatory.

On 2 February, at the Justices' monthly meeting at Preston House of Correction, Garnett talked reformatories with John Clay, and subsequently recorded long talks at Wennington Hall in the Lune valley with William Saunders, Chairman of Justices in north Lancashire, whose support had to be canvassed. At the Preston Easter Quarter Sessions the justices debated the expediency of founding a reformatory for north Lancashire. Saunders moved and Garnett seconded a motion to establish a committee to discuss the subject but it foundered among many doubts. The *Preston Guardian* had recently published a leader antagonistic to the idea on the grounds that Sunday Schools, Ragged Schools and other movements over the last 30 years had done nothing to alleviate the problems of crime, and that pressure on the parents, not the children, was the only way forward.[11] Garnett decided to go ahead on his own.

The Rev. J. Clay advised my writing to some friends to have a small preliminary meeting and talk the matter over. Half a dozen responded and met at the Bull Inn Preston on 24. v. Decided to write all round and sent out 150 copies.[12]

From this date for the rest of the year, reformatory affairs dominated Garnett's diaries almost to the exclusion of all else. Almost, but not quite. In April he recorded briefly that after talking to two influential Lancastrians about the representation of the borough, he would have no objection to being nominated for the Conservative interest. He was returned for Lancaster on 27 March 1857, and with Samuel Gregson, took his seat in April and was a useful though not distinguished member of the House for seven years, giving up in 1863 under the twin pressures of his own declining health and his father's death which left him in sole charge of the family estates.

Preparation for an election in those days of a very limited electorate did not need a great deal of work until the last minute, and throughout 1856 Garnett was very much occupied with the reformatory – drawing up his own plans, visiting as many other establishments as he could, and recruiting support. Although under the 1854 Act, part at least of the 'care and maintenance' of detainees could be covered by government funding, the physical provision of land and buildings had to be defrayed by voluntary funds. Garnett had the land on his Bleasdale estate, sour marshy land which would be returned to him in better heart from the activities of the reformatory boys. But he had to build on it, and the building he reckoned would cost £800.

The 150 letters elicited the support Garnett needed. A few dissenting voices were raised, on the grounds outlined by Thomas Eastwood (although he also promised a subscription): 'I am of opinion that to carry out such a project with success, these institutions must be supported by means of county rates.'[13] The same doubts were expressed by Jonathan Peel: 'From what I have been able to observe I am under a strong impression that the government will, ere long, be compelled to take up the subject. In such case, these small efforts may probably be found the source of much embarrassment.'[14] However, on the whole the answers were favourable and accompanied by cash. In all Garnett collected three-quarters of the sum he needed, with £100 from his father at the top of the list, as well as promises of annual subscriptions.

By this time the plans on paper were well under way. Garnett was interested in domestic design and not unskilled, having designed cottages for the Quernmore Park estate which are still comfortably lived in with minimal alterations a century and a half later. The reformatory buildings were to cater at first for 40 boys and the necessary staff, which was envisaged as a married superintendent and a single labour master. A very

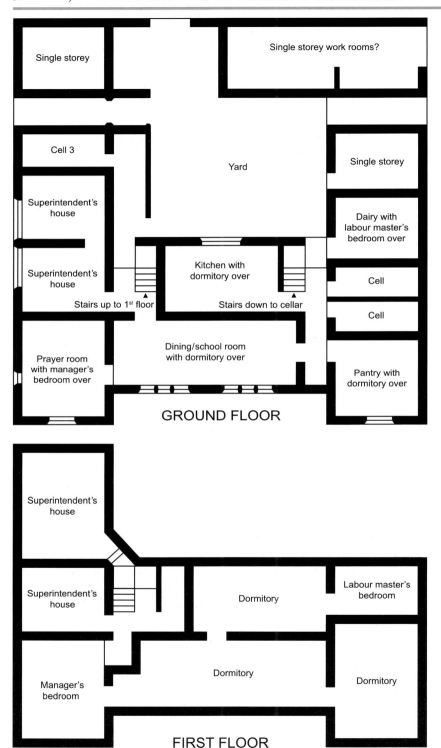

9: Reformatory Plans. Plan drawn by Simon Chew.

Single storey

Single storey work rooms?

Cell 3

Yard

Single storey

Superintendent's house

Dairy with labour master's bedroom over

Superintendent's house

Kitchen with dormitory over

Cell

Stairs up to 1st floor

Stairs down to cellar

Cell

Prayer room with manager's bedroom over

Dining/school room with dormitory over

Pantry with dormitory over

GROUND FLOOR

Superintendent's house

Superintendent's house

Dormitory

Labour master's bedroom

Manager's bedroom

Dormitory

Dormitory

FIRST FLOOR

Reformatory Plans

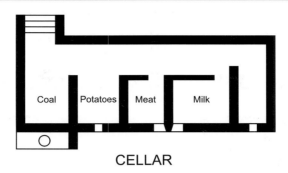

CELLAR

rough plan has survived, unfortunately unlabelled, but from various references it has been possible to reconstruct it with fair accuracy, although as the establishment grew there were many alterations and additions. The present state of the buildings, which early in the twentieth century were adapted to five dwellings within the original walls, is so complicated that it is difficult to draw many conclusions from observations on the ground.

Lloyd-Baker, whose buildings were of the simplest, was not entirely sure about the plans. He wrote in October 1856, having been kept in touch with Garnett's money-raising activities: 'I sincerely rejoice in your forwardness – only I fear you have TOO MUCH money. I don't think you CAN want it all. Only don't let it lead you to extravagance.'[15]

Sydney Turner, still the acting superintendent of the Red Hill Farm School, but soon to move to Whitehall in his new post as the first government Inspector of Reformatories, was supportive. He had urged Garnett to send him the plans as early as possible, so that any alterations could be made at an early and therefore inexpensive period, but he found little to criticise:

I like your plans in many respects extremely – recognizing in them much of that practical adaptation to the ends in view which alas our professed architects so often overlook. The only thing I do not quite like on the ground floor is mingling of the Cells with the Pantry and Dairy – but this depends a good deal on how much the Boys will be likely to pass along the passage that connects them. If, as I suspect you intend, the Boys will use the door and passage on the other side of the kitchen the objection vanishes. I hope you will not give up your first intention of Windows in the Dormitory – I have tried skylights, and found them a perpetual nuisance – specially in situations where you may expect much rain – or snow. The common window affords also far better ventilation – especially at night.[16]

The building was on a square plan, 74 feet in each direction. Inside was an open yard 42 × 34 feet, which was the boy's playground. This was entered by two opposing doors which would be securely fastened. The original sketch is not clear as to whether there was another entry to the yard, perhaps wide enough for a vehicle, on the north side opening on to the road, which at this time was a very rough cart-track. The main H-shaped building, facing south across the open country, was two-storied. It contained the large dining/schoolroom, leading on one side to the kitchen area, and on the other to a room which must be the one mentioned in Sydney Turner's first report: 'A separate room arranged for the purpose is provided for the purposes of the morning and evening worship, and when necessary for the Sunday service and instruction.'[17]

Beyond this were the superintendent's rooms which were very much integral to the structure. They had, for instance, no separate staircase; the superintendent's family would use the same stair to their bedrooms as the boys to their three dormitories, the smallest of which may have been intended as a sickroom. There was also a bedroom for a single labour-master. A room over the prayer room was kept for Garnett if he chose to stay the night, which he did during parliamentary sessions when the family was living in London. This was only from May to August each year, as his father's allowance was insufficient to rent a house in London and effectively run two establishments for the full parliamentary session. From February to April he usually stayed with his brother-in-law, Edmund Moore Q.C., who lived in Belgravia within walking distance of the House.

Under the reformatory kitchen there was a cellar, with separate compartments for coal, meat, milk and potatoes. In the kitchen passage were two narrow rooms without windows, for use as punishment cells; these were the subject of Turner's enquiry as to whether the boys would frequently pass them, which was obviously undesirable. It is clear from a diary entry when the first boys were in residence that there were three cells not two. The third one is shown at the end of the superintendent's house, reached by a fenced entry which separated it from the boys playing in the yard. The buildings on the north side of the yard are barely sketched on the original plan, but this range must have included workshops intended for the younger boys who could not be expected to work a full day on the land, and also to provide for days, of which there were plenty, when the Bleasdale weather, combined with a lack of waterproof clothing and rubber boots, prevented outdoor work. The whole building was very solid, well designed for its purpose, and not at all unhandsome. Some of the stone came from demolished farm buildings, other had to be brought in.

While the building was going forward, it was essential to find the staff. The ethos and the efficiency of a reformatory might be originally dictated by a committee as in Manchester, or an individual as at Hardwicke, but it would ultimately depend on the superintendent, who, in keeping with the thinking of the time, would live on the premises and work a 24-hour hour day in a seven-day week. Garnett's intentions with regard to such a person were impeccable, though he did not always live up to them. In a letter of November 1856 to an interested subscriber, he wrote:

> From all I have seen of such institutions and from all I hear from those practically at work with them, the resident master is the great point, and in him must rest all authority both over the subordinates and the boys, though a neighbouring gentleman may render invaluable assistance in the way of advice and direction.[18]

Garnett was fortunate in his discovery of the right man for Bleasdale, although it is clear from his diaries that he knew exactly what he wanted and worked hard to get it. Among the notes he made while staying at Hardwicke are 'Requirements of Master or Manager of the Reformatory' and these reflect Lloyd-Baker's influence:

> A good head and a kind heart both under the guiding influences of real, vital religion as exemplified in the best members of the Church of England ..... A sound discretion and tact in finding out and dealing with the characters of young boys on a system of strict but kindly discipline.

On the practical side the manager was to be as relentlessly occupied as the boys under his charge:

> A constant residence in the house and superintendence of the whole establishment keeping the accounts, journal and any other books connected with the working of the Institution ..... He will get up with the boys at 6 in the morning and instruct them in the common elements of education for about two hours every morning and the same in the evening, or thereabouts according to the season of the year: reading, writing, arithmetic and a knowledge of the Bible and catechism being essential. To dine with the boys.[19]

At the beginning of the reformatory movement there was no pool of experience, much less any training, although by the time Garnett was planning this was beginning to change. The network of managers kept each other informed of any likely candidates, and as early as April 1856 Lloyd-Baker wrote: 'By the way – I've two excellent men on hand if you want them soon – but I fear they'll be gone before you've built.'[20]

In early August 1856, before he had completed his building plans on paper, Garnett interviewed a local man called Catterall, but 'I think he is not suited to take charge of it'.[21] While in Preston three days later at the Militia Depot (he had been an enthusiastic captain in the Duke of Lancaster's Own since 1846 but had recently resigned) he sounded out a Sergeant Godkin as a suitable candidate, but nothing came of it. Later the same month, while staying at Hardwicke for the first provincial meeting of the National Reformatory Meeting, he saw Mr Cock, master of Tiverton Union School 'who is anxious to take charge of a Reformatory,' and was 'rather pleased with him and his work.'[22] On 6 September he was considering Aaron Smith who had been recommended by the Reverend Fish of the Castle Howard Reformatory: 'I shall be very thankful if he turns out to be the right one.'[23] Smith came to Bleasdale to be interviewed and on 23 September saw the foundation stone of the Reformatory laid by the elder William Garnett. He was in fact offered the post, but perhaps the bleakness of the Bleasdale surroundings deterred him and he refused the offer.

In January 1857 Garnett was staying with relations at Methley in Yorkshire and while there interviewed another possible candidate ('think he won't do'). He also visited the Wakefield House of Correction and made the acquaintance of the Governor, Mr. Shepherd ('whom I like exceedingly'), and he paid a second visit to the Calder Farm Reformatory at Mirfield. It was probably through these contacts that he heard of a possible candidate, because within ten days he went up to London, having made arrangements to meet Grant King from Redhill: 'I think him very likely to suit and made a provisional agreement with him for the situation.'[24] This move led to the first of his tiffs with Sydney Turner, who, as will be seen below, had set up a training scheme at Redhill for prospective reformatory workers, although in its first year King was the only man to apply.

Grant King was born in Buckinghamshire in 1820, the youngest child of an old yeoman family which had been established in Great Horwood for many generations. He completed a teacher training course at the Westminster Training School, and in 1843 he moved north to Armitage Bridge near Huddersfield, where he worked in two church schools. In 1848 he married a local girl, Hannah Liversidge, and they had three children, Isabella, Alfred and Emily. Hannah was also a trained teacher but taught only needlework in her husband's school. They were recommended first for both being 'communicants, and, I trust and believe, very sincere Christians.' King was judged 'an intelligent man; has his heart very much in his work; is earnest and energetic in his mode of teaching, and has power to enforce discipline. He is a little impatient, a fault not, perhaps, uncommon in very energetic persons.' His wife in her more limited role 'gave great satisfaction. Her personal appearance is good, and her habits, both at home and in the school, were neat and orderly.'[25]

King was hardly into his year at Redhill when Garnett heard of him and wrote to Sydney Turner on the subject. Turner's answer was that King was not enthusiastic, wishing to complete his training before he considered employment. However, when the two men met two days later in London, they hit it off immediately – after one lengthy conversation Garnett offered the post and King accepted, both conditional on the position at Redhill being sorted out. The liking and respect which each felt for the other at first sight never wavered over the next 16 years. King was even willing to use his own money to pay back the Treasury grant which was supporting him at Redhill and which he would have to forgo if he did not complete the training year. Garnett had not only found the man he wanted, but also a wife who shared her husband's interest and was more than willing to take on responsibilities as the school's domestic organiser and its matron, a particularly important role in the isolated back country of Bleasdale. Sydney Turner was not pleased. He tried to interest Garnett in other candidates, but to no avail; some rather acrimonious letters were exchanged, but Turner was a generous man, and his interest in the larger landscape of the reformatory movement since his promotion to government inspector led him to support the new situation and to do all he could to ensure a successful start for Bleasdale.

The building was started in September 1856. Within the year it was complete and in September 1857 it was certificated by the Home Office: 'Rather surprised, as it has not yet been inspected!'[26] Grant King had been on the payroll since June at £100 per annum plus board and lodging and laundry. This was a very respectable salary indicating the level of responsibility which went with the post (Lloyd-Baker's Bailiff was paid £30 a year). King had used the summer to complete his education by visiting as many establishments as he could manage, spent some days in September buying furniture and making ready for his family, and then went to Yorkshire to fetch them. Garnett described their arrival on 28 September:

> [they arrived] in the afternoon and took up their abode in the Reformatory, rather like a party of emigrants, and everything, of course, untidy. I had written to put them off till tomorrow, but he did not get my letter; the children having just had the scarlet fever made us more anxious about it all, however settled down tolerably well.[27]

Three weeks later the first three boys were sentenced to the Bleasdale Reformatory – by name Waddington, Entwistle and Cowan. At the time the boys were serving their preliminary sentence in the Preston House of Correction, but they arrived on 4 November, on a typically wild Bleasdale day with an east wind blowing 'from Preston, very wet, under the care of Mr. Walters and another constable. They took it very well, and seem hopeful boys. Deo Gratias.'[28] Within a fortnight, all three took off and ran back to Preston, but were caught the same day. All reformatories shared this experience: their first boys, not quite believing their luck in being out of jail, and not taking the new rules for their detention seriously, almost invariably ran away. These three were consigned to the cells on bread and water for about 48 hours, which was what would have happened to them in a real prison, and thereafter they settled down. Waddington was in trouble again in January 1858, confined to a cell for some offence, but afterwards he decided to co-operate: 'Spoke seriously to Waddington, he promises well.'[29] Two years later Waddington was the first of the Bleasdale boys to be sent out on licence.

Notes

[1]   William James Garnett (WJG), *Diary*, Jan. 1853.

[2]   WJG, *Diary*, 13 June 1854.

[3]   WJG, *Diary*, 4 Oct. 1844.

[4]   Lloyd-Baker, T.B., Letter to WJG, LRO, DDQ 7/46/1.

[5]   Lloyd-Baker, Letter, LRO, DDQ 7/46/2.

[6]   WJG, Notebook, LRO, DDQ 7/48/6.

[7]   Ibid.

[8]   Ibid.

[9]   Lloyd-Baker, Letter to *Leeds Mercury*, 27 Nov. 1854.

[10]   WJG, Notebook.

[11]   *Preston Guardian*, 9 April 1856.

[12]   WJG, Notebook.

[13]   Eastwood, T., letter to WJG, LRO, DDQ 7/49/30.

[14]   Peel, J., Letter to WJG, LRO, DDQ 7/49/31.

[15]   Lloyd-Baker, Letter to WJG, LRO, DDQ 7/46/7.

[16]   Turner, S., Letter to WJG, LRO, DDQ 7/48/13.

[17]   Inspector of Reformatories, *Annual Report*, 1858.

[18]   WJG, Letter, LRO, DDQ 7/49/71.

[19]   WJG, Notebook.

[20]   Lloyd-Baker, Letter to WJG, LRO, DDQ 7/46/5.

[21]   WJG, *Diary*, 2 Aug. 1856.

[22]   WJG, *Diary*, 22 Aug. 1856.

[23]   WJG, *Diary*, 6 Sept. 1856.

[24]   WJG, *Diary*, 9 Feb. 1857.

[25]   Letter to WJG, LRO, DDQ 7/48/14.

[26]   WJG, *Diary*, 6 Sept. 1857.

[27]   WJG, *Diary*, 28 Sept. 1857.

[28]   WJG, *Diary*, 4 Nov. 1857.

[29]   WJG, *Diary*, 5 Jan. 1858.

CHAPTER FOUR

Bleasdale Reformatory (1857–1869)

The early history of Bleasdale Reformatory is both more and less detailed than that of other Lancashire reformatories – the available sources being completely different. No official records have been discovered, apart from the inspector's brief annual reports, the census returns, and one or two articles in the local press concerning untoward incidents. William James Garnett's first thoughts included the establishment of a committee of management, and in other areas of his life, both political and judicial, he was a good committee man. But after the failed attempt to engage the practical interest of local magistrates, and under the influence of Thomas Barwick Lloyd-Baker and John Clay, both of whom worked in a highly personal fashion, Bleasdale never had a committee. There are therefore, no committee minutes or other official documents to consult. When Garnett was unable to keep an eye on the place, because he was in London during parliamentary sessions, and later because his declining health sent him to the south of France for the winter months, he relied almost entirely on Grant King the superintendent. Thomas Cranston, his estate agent, had a supervisory role with regard to finance, and Garnett's close friend, Charles Roger Jacson of Barton, held a watching brief over the general running of the place, and audited the accounts.

The two chief sources of information on the Bleasdale Reformatory are Garnett's own diaries (he kept a diary all his adult life and hardly ever missed an entry)[1] and the letters which Grant King wrote regularly to keep him advised of the smallest particulars of the running of the place, and to seek permission for anything out of the ordinary.[2] Apart from significant expenditure on the farm or the buildings, this at first mainly involved those areas where the reformatory interacted with the outside world – the acceptance or rejection of boys, their exeats on holiday and their licensing to the world of work. Nearly 300 of these letters have survived, and Grant King must have written more than this. There are not only considerable gaps, but the diaries show where these coincided with Garnett's absences from home, during which he expected to be kept apprised of events, and there are occasional direct references in the diaries to letters received which are no longer in the collection.

For the first few months of the establishment, from November 1857, there are no letters, for the obvious reason that Garnett, from his home a few hundred yards away, was in and out sometimes more than once in the day. From April 1858, when he took up his seat in Parliament, until the end of 1859, the letters provide a valuable resource detailing the establishment and expansion of the fledgling reformatory. Regrettably, those for the next four years have been lost. The series starts again towards the end of 1863, by which time Garnett was no longer living at Bleasdale, and they continue somewhat spasmodically until a few months before his death in 1873. He was then a very sick man, and the letters stop at almost the same moment that he gave up making diary entries.

One of the main responsibilities which Garnett at first kept in his own hands was the selection of his young criminals. It was desirable to catch and reform boys before it was too late. It was also desirable to break up gangs by removing the ringleaders. All reformatories wanted to have boys young enough, and with a long enough sentence, for them to be subject to a reasonable spell in the school and a further spell under licence.

Many managers did not want first convictions, and Garnett was of this party which followed Lloyd-Baker's lead in being strongly against using reformatory sentences for such youngsters: 'A first conviction is no sign of criminal habits .... I believe the greater part of the population have at some time while young taken something that did not belong to them.'[3] Garnett canvassed opinion and preserved some of the answers. Ishmael Fish of Castle Howard wrote: 'My Committee have decided to take no more first convictions, but many of our friends think us in the wrong.'[4] Wheatley Balme of Calder Farm was not so sure, pointing out that first convictions did not necessarily represent first offences: 'With us, I think a boy has generally been several times guilty before people harden their hearts to take him before a magistrate.'[5] But Lloyd-Baker was strongly of the opposite point of view

> unless it is fully understood and rigidly carried out – that Reformatories are to be used not to save the Poor Rate – not to save the Clergyman or the Schoolmaster some little trouble by ridding them of a boy that will make a noise and won't do what he is ordered – Not even as a charity to help at the national expense some man who is very poor and lives in "such a dirty cottage" – But – To check a boy at the moment that he is entering a course of habitual crime.[6]

Bleasdale tried to follow the rule, but there were always exceptions. An inspector's report comments 'Mr Garnett declines to admit boys on their first commitment, except in very special cases. Out of the 19 boys admitted in 1860, six were of this class.'[7] Six out of 19 seems rather more than 'very special' but the pressure from magistrates about which Lloyd-Baker complained was probably heavy on all reformatories, particularly as the managers themselves were magistrates who had to negotiate with their own friends and acquaintance.

There was no disagreement about the fact that the keystone of all reformatory treatment was hard physical work, as Grant King expressed in one of his early letters.

> I feel still more convinced that we are right to introduce work as one of the chief agents in the Reformatory: when I say work, I mean real, hard work, as hard as that performed by common labourers, and nearly, if not quite, as long continued.[8]

Bleasdale Reformatory was built in an area of sour mossland, and over the years boy labour was used to dig, trench, drain and where possible make it productive. There was nothing strange at the period in making 14-year-olds work like men – they did so in the outside world, and in this as everything else it had to be abundantly clear that reformatory boys were not better treated than their honest counterparts. To some of them, who came from the coal pits, there would have been no great shock, but a good number (20 out of 46 in the 1861 census) had only experience of the warm, damp, enervating atmosphere of the cotton mills, and the transition to outdoor work must have been severe. None-the-less the system seems to have worked well, as the Bleasdale health record was second to none. However, one would give much to have a boy's-eye view of the place and his treatment.

Once the place had settled down, absconding was a fairly minor problem. Some boys ran away out of devilment and a longing for adventure, and although discipline demanded that they be punished, references seem to show that their very naughtiness seemed hopeful. One such was David Thompson, a small Scottish lad who absconded at least three times. The first time Garnett noted in his diary 'brought back this afternoon by Mr Superintendent Greene. Determined not to send him to prison.'[9] Within two weeks he was off again: 'Disturbed by the Scotch boy, David Thompson, running away again from the Reformatory; heard of his going over the fell towards Calder. Endeavoured to catch him but in vain. What a silly, stupid boy.'[10] It is not recorded how long he was free this time, but the 'silly, stupid boy' sounds like exasperation, because if such escapades continued there would be no option but prison.

By the next summer Thompson had clearly found expression for his energy in more law-abiding ways. King wrote to Garnett: 'Our best little worker – Thompson – broke his arm yesterday.' He was working at the bridge and got his arm caught between two wagons being used to convey materials on the steep slope. 'I do not think any blame could be attached to any one, except that the little fellow's determination to stop the waggon when his strength was not sufficient put him in danger.' They hustled him down to Mr Chapman, the apothecary at Garstang, to have it set and put in a sling, but he was not in the least sorry for himself:

10: The Bridge at Bleasdale. Photograph by Angus Winchester, 2007.

He was up as soon as any of the rest and his love of employment has perhaps shown itself more sharply than ever for all the morning or at any rate the most part of it, he was taking clothes from the mangle with his right hand, keeping his left in a sling. He is now standing with the masons, I see.[11]

Six months later in the middle of winter, he absconded again with another boy. 'Extraordinary'[12] commented Garnett, but there are no further references to him until the end of 1865, by which time Thompson was in India with his battalion of the Sherwood Foresters. King had had a letter from another ex-Bleasdale boy 'and he tells me that he has seen David Thompson the little Scotch Run-a-way, who is also in India in the 45th Regiment, and when Price wrote he was ill in the fever and wished Price to mention him to me.'[13] As there is no trace of David Thompson's name in the regimental books or discharge papers, it is probable that he died in India, then or later, as did so many ordinary soldiers who succumbed in that unforgiving climate to fever, drink or syphilis.

A new venture tends to succeed because at first everyone is engaged in getting it off the ground, and this builds strong bonds between them. The good spirit at Bleasdale, often commented on by the inspectors, must have been strongly fostered by their first big communal enterprise, the building of the bridge, which has been mentioned as the scene of David Thompson's accident.

The road which leads past the reformatory, up the fell to the farm of Hazelhurst and then round in a loop to Admarsh church, was at the time

a very rough track. A hundred yards west of the reformatory it crossed the Clough Heads Brook. Garnett saw an opportunity: 'Gave orders about taking down the old bridge at Clough Edge, and prepared for rebuilding it with Chris Foster [the labour master] and the boys at the Reformatory. Some offer very well as masons.'[14]

The building of the bridge took a year to complete, and by any standards is a fine piece of work. It fills the ravine with a handsome arch, and the road now runs on the level, at least six metres above the stream. By the time the bridge was completed, the reformatory population had reached 33, but not all the boys worked on the bridge, and probably none of them all the time. One of the stars of the project was the boy called Waddington, one of the first three to arrive in November 1857, and twice an absconder. As it is unlikely that Garnett would have accepted in the very first batch anyone over the age of 15, he cannot have been more than 17 when King noted in June 1859: 'Waddington has nearly finished dressing the coping of the bridge.'[15]

The bridge stands as good as new after 150 years, and it is extremely hard to believe that any of it, perhaps particularly the meticulously cut coping stones, was done by untrained boy labour. The labour master, Christopher Foster, may or may not have been a trained mason, but he seems to have been one who could get the very best from his young workforce. In June he was asking Garnett's permission for Waddington to carve a stone on the upstream face of the bridge recording their achievement. The stone is set very high, and much lichened, but has been recently read as: 'This Bridge BEGUN August 17 1858 FINISHED 1859.

W[a]s Bu[ilt by] the BOYS of The Bleasdale Reformatory School Grant King Governor Christopher Foster Mason Instructor.'[16] On the downstream side another stone is carved with the dividers, hammer and other mason's tools.

12: Bleasdale Reformatory Uniform Button. Photograph by Angus Winchester, 2008.

The bridge was finished in August, and a couple of months later Waddington was out on licence, the first to be taken in, and the first to be sent out. Garnett noted: 'The last Sunday there for E. Waddington, who goes out on trial tomorrow to work in Blackburn; he went to church in his new clothes – an interesting evening.' And the next day: 'E Waddington went down with me in the morning and on from Preston to Blackburn. I hope he may do well, our first boy sent out.'[17]

It is apparent from the inspector's reports that in all reformatories industrial work took priority over education, and Bleasdale was no exception. School was scheduled for the early hours before breakfast and in the evening after the physical work was over. It was hard for boys who had been up since 5.30 and had done six hours work in the open air to be at their mental best. Even so, in the first years, with Grant King himself as the only teacher, the results were good: 'The school instruction did not satisfy me so well' was Turner's criticism in 1863, when the numbers had risen to nearly 60:

> I attribute the falling off to the want of a sufficient staff, Mr Grant King having on his hands the whole of the school teaching as well as of the industrial and superintendence, an amount of labour and responsibility which, with all his ability and zeal, he could hardly be equal to carry on.[18]

This year saw the recruitment of the first of a number of teaching assistants, who came and went and showed none of the stability of the labour masters, who tended to be older married men with their own families.

A good example of the latter was John Kenyon the tailor, who worked at the reformatory, as far as can be ascertained, for seven years 1858–1865. He was perhaps a good choice as a practical example of modest success from an unpromising start. A poor boy from West Derby who came to Chipping, probably to Brabin's Charity School, and from there was apprenticed to a Chipping tailor, Kenyon was appointed to the reformatory, married a local girl and raised a family. Tradition has it that they lived at the Bleasdale lodge gates, remote from the reformatory complex, where the children were frightened at night by the owls hooting in the dark. An account book shows that when the number of boys

13: John Kenyon.
Photograph
reproduced by
permission of Mrs
Muriel Lord, copied
by Angus Winchester.

increased to a level sufficient to keep the tailor's shop running full time, making not only the boys' uniforms, but clothes for the Garstang workhouse and other customers. Kenyon earned 16 shillings a week and a commission on sales, making up about £50 a year. He had a free house and may also have drawn supplies from the reformatory. When he left in 1865 to set up his own tailor's shop in Chipping, Kenyon's two sons followed him as master tailors.[19]

The struggle to make the workshops and the farm financially viable was as high on King's list of priorities as on that of his manager: every year's end showing a gap which had to be filled from Garnett's private funds. To do them both justice, they did not cut corners in their

14: Bleasdale Lodge. Photograph by Angus Winchester, 2007.

provision for the boys, but they did work very hard towards profitability, as many references in the letters show. The boys' education was the loser. However King, after the manner of teachers at all times, was not above indulging in a burst of classroom activity just before the inspector's visit: 'This haytime we are leaving off work at 4.30 to give a little more time for school work, as I should like the boys to be fairly intelligent in their examination by Mr Turner.'[20]

From the beginning it was Grant King's gift to foster a spirit of trust between himself and his boys. [He] 'has been very successful in maintaining discipline, and at the same time establishing a cheerful natural tone of feeling among them.'[21] The atmosphere of the place can be illustrated by the story of the lost key which occurred in May 1859 – at a time when there were still no more than 25 boys in the school. A boy from Halifax, Kershaw by name, stole one of the dormitory keys off the ring and hid it in the fireplace of his dormitory, but it slipped down between the bricks and he could not get it out again. In fact, it would have been no use to him as the dormitory was secured at night from the outside. The thief was not discovered at first, and the building was turned upside down to find the lost key:

The other boys I may say felt the disgrace most acutely and I am glad to say tried all in their power to discover the culprit ..... I wish you could have seen Holt, Guy and Morris last Sunday morning overturning almost everything in the woodshed with earnest, anxious faces, of their own accord too, while I was at breakfast, looking for the key. In fact on Wednesday night after Kershaw had publicly given me the key, Holt said when I went into the bedroom – "Well, I am glad the key is found, for I have not felt gradely since it was lost till now". If we can but keep a good majority on the right side, success will not, I feel certain, be doubtful.[22]

Physical punishment was of course used, but not very often. No punishment book has survived but the cells are only mentioned in cases of absconding. The reformatory had been running for a year and a half when King reported:

I have had the first case of wanton mischief that I have known today. Hesketh, Greenwood and young Haddock while employed in chopping sticks this morning in the shed, employed themselves very foolishly in cutting each other's caps. I intend to send them upstairs when they come in this evening into separate bedrooms and give each a caning – Hesketh and Greenwood rather sharply as both of them are of a bad stamp.[23]

Such comments are not frequent. A critic might say that the letters are obviously selective, being written from an employee to his employer, but the tone of them clearly shows that King welcomed every chance to share his problems with his manager: 'I am sorry you could not come down as your presence seems like such a support to me, even when things are going on well as they are at present.'[24] The language in which King referred to his boys was normally positive and indeed affectionate. More than once he commented that discipline was no problem:

57 in the house; no difficulty in managing them; this you will be glad of as the bad case of open rebellion at Castle Howard will make many friends of Reformatories quite uneasy. I believe that as long as lads see and know that they are treated justly and that all the dealings with them are open and above board, they will render a cheerful obedience to those who are over them. At any rate, such has been the case here. I never had a really saucy answer from any lad, nor any act of determined disobedience, neither need any of the men if they have sense enough to talk little and quietly show a lad what they want him to do.[25]

The first death on the premises did not occur until 1867, and King was much affected. He could not put pen to paper until five days later: 'it has made me so busy and to a certain extent uncomfortable.' Boys were working unsupervised at bringing cartloads of stones down the hill from the quarry and a big lad insisted on riding, in spite of the little horseboy's attempts to stop him. The cart overturned and he was killed instantly:

> We buried him on Monday, and his mother and three sisters came over to his funeral .... Mr Barclay [the incumbent] came over on Monday and was present at the inquest and walked with us all to Church. All the boys followed and I believe there was not one eye dry in the school while all stood to hear Isabella play the dead March in Saul just before we removed the coffin from the school. We furnished every lad – 70 – with a black tie.[26]

Bleasdale did not adopt the system used in some reformatories of using food as an incentive to good behaviour. They preferred monetary awards, first noted at Hardwicke. Boys were issued with savings books, and their good marks totted up into small amounts of money which were handed over when they left. As a positive incentive, it was frequently praised by the inspectors who wished that more reformatories would adopt it.

The boys were well though monotonously fed. No dietary sheet has survived, but an elaborate sheet of monitors' duties from 1870 shows boys detailed to serve bread, baked pudding, milk, potatoes, porridge, rice, cocoa, soup, meat and cheese.[27] 'Plenty of work, plenty to eat and quite enough play, as one of them told his parents in a letter the other day.'[28] As a staple, rather than bread there was heavy reliance on oatmeal porridge both for breakfast and supper, but this was nothing unusual in a north-country district, and in one of his later disagreements with Sydney Turner, who queried the diet, Garnett retorted 'that the cost of a dietary is by no means a test of its nutrition; our oatmeal porridge is far better than many things which cost more money; we don't approve in the north of south country slops.'[29] It is worth remarking that as late as the 1940s local farm men ate a basin full of oatmeal 'poddish' for breakfast and supper, followed by tea out of the same basin.[30]

The garden supplied vegetables. After a very dry spell in the spring and summer of 1859, which badly delayed the crops, King remarked in one of his letters:

> Our potatoes are now beginning to look up though we shall have to wait for a considerable time before our earliest ones are fit to dig. Another year I hope we shall manage better for potatoes and different kinds of greens, as nothing is more conducive to health than a free supply of greens and other vegetables.[31]

On another occasion there was a glut, and King reported buying: '11 flitches of American bacon to be able to use more potatoes as they are so cheap.'[32] An interesting social comment is provided by a later letter

Calder Farm School
Diet Tables

	No. 1 — 1st under 11 years			No. 2 — Ordinary		
	Breakfast	Dinner	Supper	Breakfast	Dinner	Supper
Monday	1/2 pint of thick water & 8 oz of Bread	1 pint of Broth / 2 oz of Meat / & 8 oz of Bread	1 pint of Cocoa & 8 oz of Bread	1/2 pint of Milk & Water & 8 oz of Bread	1 pint of Broth & 8 oz of Bread	1 pint of Cocoa & 8 oz of Bread
Tuesday	Do	1 lb of suet pudding	Do	Do	2 oz of Cheese & 8 oz of Bread	Do
Wednesday	Do	1 pint of Broth / 2 oz of Meat / & 8 oz of Bread	Do	Do	1 pint of Broth & 8 oz of Bread	Do
Thursday	Do	1 lb of Potatoes / 2 oz of Meat / & 8 oz of Bread	Do	Do	1 lb of Potatoes / 2 oz of Meat / & 8 oz of Bread	Do
Friday	Do	6 oz of Rice (boiled) a little butter & 8 oz of Bread	Do	Do	6 oz of Rice (boiled) & 8 oz of Bread	Do
Saturday	Do	3 oz of Cheese or a little butter & 8 oz of Bread	Do	Do	2 oz of Cheese & 8 oz of Bread	Do
Sunday	1/2 pint of Milk & Water 8 oz of Bread & a little butter or dripping	4 oz of Meat & 8 oz of Bread	1 pint of Cocoa 8 oz of Bread a little butter or dripping	1/2 pint of Milk & Water 8 oz of Bread & a little butter or dripping	4 oz of Meat & 8 oz of Bread	1 pint of Cocoa 8 oz of Bread a little butter or dripping

The 1/2 pint of Milk & Water contains a pint of skim milk.
The cocoa is made with 1/2 oz of flake cocoa to the pint.

The cook is made on the Broth from Sunday's meat with Carrots, Turnips, Onions & pease added. The soup on Wednesday contains meat also.

15: Calder Vale Diet Sheet. Reproduced with the kind permission of the depositor and the County Archivist, Lancashire Record Office. Ref. DDQ/7/49/75.

concerning tinned Australian mutton which as early as 1870 was evidently cheaper than buying meat in Garstang market: 'about 6d per lb if ten cases, each containing twelve canisters of 6 or 7 lbs each are taken at one time ... You will see there are plain directions for cooking it: perhaps the cheapest and best way is in soup or hash.'[33]

Nevertheless on the subject of diet Sydney Turner had some wise words to say in a letter to Garnett:

> In your general principle that Boys in a Reformatory should not be made better off than the ordinary class of poor and unconvicted lads around them, I fully agree – It is a doctrine I have always preached and stuck to in practice. But it must be acted on with the reservation that in both diet and recreation some extra allowance must be made to counteract the depressing influence of the long confinement and monotonous routine of food, employment etc which detention for 3,4 or 5 years involves. We know how the absence of free life acts on Prisoners and we see the same in the Industrial Schools. The Child who thrives and grows on a crust in the gutter dwindles and droops when taken to the school and made a regular boarder there tho' of course fed and clothed much better than he was on the streets.[34]

The monotony at Bleasdale was in fact reasonably well broken, the remoteness of the place making it possible to allow the boys more freedom than those in the city reformatories. The boys were not dragooned all the time: there was no formal escort for boys going up to the Tower to work in the gardens, down to the school or the vicarage to deliver letters, or to a farm to help in the hayfield. It is clear that King believed in treats, not least because such breaks were as welcome to the staff as the boys. The staff worked long hours with little respite. It was not until 1865 that King asked permission for a beer and tea allowance for them – and it was not until 1867 that he was able to fix up some sort of staff room:

> I am very anxious to fit up a room for the men to dine and use as a reading room and they are willing to subscribe to a daily paper: we think of taking the Standard: if you have any very old pictures or periodicals, that you can spare, I shall be glad to make use of them.[35]

Against that spartan background small pleasures loomed large. From time to time in the summer the whole school had an outing on the moors:

> We went over the Fells to your shooting hut in the Calder Valley yesterday afternoon and returned by the Paper Mill. Mrs King, C. Foster [the labour master], Mrs Foster, Mr Kenyon [the tailor],

Richard and George Billington [the gamekeeper and his son] were with us and all of us certainly enjoyed the scenery very much indeed. The weather was delightful and most of the boys had a good bathe in the river.[36]

Expeditions to the hut became a feature of the summer months, sometimes at Whitsun and sometimes as a celebration of 'Harvest Home'. In the early years Garnett joined in:

The weather being fine, after post time, the reformatory holiday, and all went over to the Hut, a party of 70; Mr King and all his family, Chr. Foster and all his, Messrs Kenyon and Hoyle and 56 boys; there by 12, over the fells, sang songs, psalms and harvest hymns, boiled coffee and potatoes etc, and all as happy as possible; I enjoyed it immensely.[37]

There was of course a Christmas dinner, usually on Boxing Day, and some kind of New Year treat. 'I shall carry out your wishes on Epiphany day' King wrote to Garnett when the latter was in the South of France:

... and if fine the boys shall have half a holiday and perhaps take a stroll in the hills.[38]..... I gave the boys a good treat of oranges and Spanish Juice [liquorice] on Monday December 26th which day they had their roast beef and plum pudding. I never saw them enjoy themselves more. The singing on Xmas Day at church was really of a cheerful character. We took the Harmonium and Isabella played. We chanted the psalms and made a really joyful day of it.[39]

Music in the form of choral singing was a feature of the place, mainly because it was one of King's interests. To fill a gap he would often give the boys an hour's vigorous singing practice, and there are many requests to Garnett to send him some more, and different, pieces: 'More interesting matter for our singing when used as recreation and in play hours on wet days.'[40] After the first 18 months, the monotony was further broken by boys being allowed home on leave. This may have had a divisive as well as a cheering effect because permission probably depended not only on good conduct but also on the home background being suitable. Some boys were clearly aware of the possibility of being drawn back into bad old ways. 'Rostron who is going to Preston' wrote Grant King, 'begs that Cowan may not be allowed to go at the same time.'[41] The standard allowance seems to have been quite generous, usually from Saturday morning until the following Wednesday or Thursday. How, or if, it was arranged for boys whose homes were not in Lancashire is not clear. There is no record of a boy not returning at the appointed time, even if he left it as late as possible and had to face a five-mile walk in the midsummer twilight: 'Holt came home all right about 11 1/2 last night – he reached the Garstang Station at 10. He seems in excellent spirits after his journey home.'[42]

Thirteen-year-old James Whitworth wrote up his version of his holiday and Grant King was sufficiently impressed to send the sheet to Garnett to see, adding honestly that the spelling had been improved a little from the original version:

> The first words my Aunt said to me when she had asked me how long I had to stop were that I had improved in my schooling very much and she was pleased with me and my Father praised me very much and all that know me. Mr Atkins told my father that he would take me for to work for him when my time was up and when I went to see him he gave me a shilling and told me to try to improve this year as much as I had the last and he would have taken me then if my time had been up.[43]

There must have been some rules for limiting personal possessions, but these seem to have been fairly easy, and King was amused to note the choice of articles brought back by different boys from their exeat: 'McCloud's included writing paper, stamped envelopes, new handkerchief, straw hat for himself and one for Waddington, hair oil and a square of scented soap.'[44]

An important part of the reformatory's work was placing the boys at the end of their sentence, and at first Bleasdale did not rate highly with Sydney Turner:

> Mr. King is both able and zealous, and does not spare exertion, but no one man can satisfactorily discharge the various duties connected with the management of nearly 60 boys, taking an active part in their school instruction and out-door employment, and at the same time devote the time and attention to their disposal, and their conduct and circumstance after discharge, which are required to make a reformatory thoroughly successful.[45]

The situation improved later, particularly when Alfred was old enough to be taken on as his father's assistant, but it was never easy. A disadvantage of the reformatory training was the emphasis on agricultural work, which was inappropriate to the industrial background from which most of the boys came. Some indeed elected to stay in the country: 'You will be glad to hear that Moores has got a situation at Mr Smith's at Sandholm Mill at £7 for the first year, with board, lodging, washing and mending same as other farm servants.'[46] However, most not unnaturally wanted to go home, and not all families were able or willing to offer the stable and respectable background which was required: 'Hoyle .... can if he will do well, but I don't think he can with his own folks – boaters at Warrington.'[47] Grant King may not have had the time or the staff always to do this part of his job properly, especially considering that many boys came from further afield than Lancashire, but there is no doubt of the interest he took in them. 'Do you think the New Zealand emigration agent would help us in Whittaker's case, and let us get him off first – his parents are in really good circumstances there and the only question is how to get the youth over to them.'[48]

Emigration had been seen as a hopeful outcome for many delinquent youngsters since Edward Brenton's pioneering work with the Children's Friend Society, 30 years before. A certain number of Bleasdale boys are reported as going to Canada. James Whitworth, who wrote his little essay about a successful home leave was one of the first. The details available about this boy make a rather odd patchwork. King first mentioned him to Garnett very early in the life of the reformatory, asking permission to accept him: 'His case appears to be exactly such a one as a Reformatory is intended to meet.'[49] What this means is not clear, but probably that his family was a respectable one which had nevertheless lost control of him. The parents were married, and had two other children besides James. The boy was taken before the Salford Petty Sessions in March 1858, his crime being recorded as that of stealing one penny from his father George, for which he was given 60 days in jail, a whipping and three years reformatory. One has to presume that his father colluded with the legal authorities to get him arrested and given such a sentence. From the available details, he seems to have been 12 years old at the time. He settled well at Bleasdale, and, as noted above, was one of the first to go out on home leave, reporting back that his family was pleased with his progress. In November 1859 Garnett recorded in his diary that Whitworth was one of two boys to be baptised at Admarsh Chapel, which the register confirms. This is odd, as he had been baptised as an infant at Manchester Cathedral in January 1846: son of George Whitworth of Salford, a joiner, and his wife Ann. In July 1861, aged about 16, he had completed his sentence and was one of the first two boys to opt for emigration. Garnett, who was in London for the parliamentary session, travelled to Liverpool to see them off:

> By 6.15 train to Liverpool to see the two boys, Whitworth and Davies, embark for Canada by the "Hibernian" steamship. Found them at the office at 12.30 to 1 p.m., paid the passage money £12 and settled all for them, saw them on board the steam tender at 4 and returned to London by 5 ock train home 11.20 p.m. a long day's work and rather tired.[50]

The *Hibernian* and other emigrant ships shuttled back and forth across the Atlantic during the summer and autumn months, carrying hundreds of steerage passengers on each voyage. The *Hibernian*, carrying about 360, was by no means one of the largest. She could expect in reasonable weather to take 11 days in transit to Quebec, and might make eight such transits in the season. One of the advantages of emigration for those boys who opted for it was that their agricultural training stood them in good stead. It is unclear what kind of agency existed at the far end to find places for reformatory boys, and to some extent keep an eye on them; the system at this stage seems to have been much less than perfect. Research in Canada has failed to find any trace of Whitworth settling there for good. However, the 1881 census for Salford shows a James Whitworth of the right age married and working in the iron works, so it is more than a fair guess that he returned home after a while and settled in his native town.

Another Bleasdale boy who by chance is quite well documented had a chequered career in the reformatory. Copping appears on the scene in January 1864. King reported him as going on 'steadily and well' and he seems to have been a monitor, helping with the little boys who made paper bags for the Oakenclough paper mill. King spoke too soon: three weeks later Copping absconded with two others; they got up early to light the kitchen fire and by six o'clock had disappeared into the dark. It was April before King was able to report 'We have got Copping back but not his partners; he has had quite a romantic affair.' The three had made for Carlisle, and when there had gone to the police for tickets for a night's lodging. These were handed out without question 'with my description in the office, stating that the soles of their shoes were marked BRS.' At Carlisle he was separated from one companion, travelled to Newcastle, and lost the other.

Copping crossed to Stockton-on-Tees on his own, and then, working his way south, was caught up in the great Dale Dyke Dam disaster at Sheffield:

> Then to Sheffield where he says he narrowly escaped drowning – lived with some workpeople and worked at sword-polishing – both the man and his wife and two children are drowned – Copping got on a raft or something of the kind and was taken out of the river at Chesterfield. He then made for London, where his uncle, (a superannuated police officer) gave him up to police.[51]

Copping no doubt had his turn in the cells for this long escapade, but there seems to have been no question of sending him to gaol, and he settled down. A year later he was again in a trusted position: 'You will be glad to hear that I have no trouble in the Reformatory; in fact the work of managing the boys never seemed easier. Copping helps well, and so does Read the Labour Monitor.'[52] But a few weeks later, after a home leave, he absconded again:

> .... [his] term here expires next August and the question is shall we be at the expense of his capture? For the sake of example he should be

caught but to himself no good will arise, I imagine, as if after all the kindness shown to him he is base enough to act in such a sneakish manner, no instruction or reproof either will be of much avail.[53]

Whether Copping came back or not is not recorded, but at the end of his reformatory sentence he was again in touch with Bleasdale, and King had quite forgiven him. In October of 1866, King wrote: 'I am glad to inform you that C. Copping has succeeded in getting the second mastership of a ragged school in Manchester.'[54] In December, visiting Manchester: 'I also saw C. Copping, who appears to be going on very well. I went to the school where he acts as assistant and his master speaks very well of him in every respect.'[55] A few months later: 'Copping has just got a situation as schoolmaster at Leek workhouse in Staffordshire at £30 per an. with Rations etc.'[56] And there, unfortunately, the trail goes cold.

It is in the nature of the Bleasdale material that although it delivers a series of vivid snapshots of a kind unrivalled in the documentation of any of the early Lancashire reformatories, they remain as snapshots, and the broader questions go unanswered. In particular one would like to know how successful the regime was in turning round the lives of its boys and sending them out able and willing to fit into an ordinary industrious working life.

Notes

[1] The diaries are in private hands.

[2] LRO, DDQ 7/50/1–266.

[3] Lloyd-Baker, T.B., Letter to WJG, 21 June 1859, LRO, DDQ 7/46/14.

[4] Fish, I., Letter to WJG, 26 Dec. 1857, LRO, DDQ 7/49/73.

[5] Wheatley Balme, Letter to WJG, 29 Dec. 1857, LRO, DDQ 7/49/73.

[6] Lloyd-Baker Letter to WJG, 22 Dec. 1857, LRO, DDQ 7/49/73.

[7] Inspector of Reformatories, *Annual Report*, 1860.

[8] Grant King (GK) Letter to WJG, 15 May 1858, LRO, DDQ 7/50/8.

[9] WJG, *Diary*, 15 Aug. 1858.

[10] WJG, *Diary*, 28 Aug. 1858.

[11] GK Letter to WJG, 8 June 1859, LRO, DDQ 7/50/15.

[12] WJG, *Diary*, 7 Jan. 1860.

[13] GK Letter to WJG, 20 Dec. 1865, LRO, DDQ 7/50/76.

[14] WJG, *Diary*, 17 Sept. 1858.

[15] GK Letter to WJG, 3 June 1859, LRO, DDQ 7/30/11.

[16] Information from Mrs Muriel Lord of Chipping.

[17] WJG, *Diary*, 30–31 Oct. 1859.

[18] Inspector of Reformatories *Annual Report*, 1863.

[19] Information from Mrs Muriel Lord of Chipping.

20   GK Letter to WJG, 21 June 1859, LRO, DDQ 7/50/23.

21   Inspector of Reformatories *Annual Report*, 1859.

22   GK Letters to WJG, 14–15 May 1858, LRO, DDQ 7/50/7–8.

23   GK Letter to WJG, 21 June 1859, LRO, DDQ 7/50/23.

24   GK Letter to WJG, 2 July 1859, LRO, DDQ 7/50/28.

25   GK Letter to WJG, 29 April 1864, LRO, DDQ 7/50/58.

26   GK Letter to WJG, 13 March 1867, LRO, DDQ 7/50/110.

27   LRO, DDQ 7/49/76.

28   GK Letter to WJG, 8 May 1858, LRO, DDQ 7/49/20.

29   WJG Letter to S. Turner, LRO, DDQ 7/49/20.

30   Information from Mrs Muriel Lord of Chipping.

31   GK Letter to WJG, 4 July 1859, LRO, DDQ 7/50/29.

32   GK Letter to WJG, 4 March 1864, LRO, DDQ 7/50/54.

33   GK Letter to WJG, 23 Aug. 1870, LRO, DDQ 7/50/190.

34   Turner, S., Letter to WJG, 8 June 1870, LRO DDQ 7/49/20.

35   GK Letter to WJG, 26 Dec. 1867, LRO, DDQ 7/50/126.

36   GK Letter to WJG, 26 June 1859, LRO, DDQ 7/50/25.

37   WJG, *Diary*, 10 Oct. 1862.

38   GK Letter to WJG, 1 Jan. 1865, LRO, DDQ 7/50/48.

39   GK Letter to WJG, 5 Jan. 1865, LRO, DDQ 7/50/59.

40   GK Letter to WJG, 4 June 1859, LRO, DDQ 7/50/13.

41   GK Letter to WJG, 1 June 1859, LRO, DDQ 7/50/11.

42   GK Letter to WJG, 23 June 1859, LRO, DDQ 7/50/24.

43   James Whitworth Essay, June 1859, LRO,DDQ 7/50/28.

44   GK Letter to WJG, 2 July 1859, LRO, DDQ 7/50/28.

45   Inspector of Reformatories *Annual Report*, 1864.

46   GK Letter to WJG, 29 April 1864, LRO, DDQ 7/50/58.

47   GK Letter to WJG, 8 April 1864, LRO, DDQ 7/50/57.

48   GK Letter to WJG, 3 Aug. 1865, LRO, DDQ 7/50/67.

49   GK Letter to WJG, 5 May 1858, LRO, DDQ 7/50/3.

50   WJG, *Diary*, 4 July 1861.

51   GK Letter to WJG, 8 April 1864, LRO, DDQ 7/50/57.

52   GK Letter to WJG, 10 Oct.1865, LRO, DDQ 7/50/73.

53   GK Letter to WJG, 27 Jan. 1866, LRO, DDQ 7/50/79.

54   GK Letter to WJG, 24 Oct. 1866, LRO, DDQ 7/50/97.

55   GK Letter to WJG, 3 Dec. 1866, LRO, DDQ 7/50/106.

56   GK Letter to WJG, 9 April 1867, LRO, DDQ 7/50/113.

CHAPTER FIVE

Bleasdale Reformatory (1870–1880)

From the first three boys who arrived on that rain-soaked day in November 1857 Bleasdale grew steadily though not rapidly in numbers, and by 1861 the inspector's report showed a roll of 47 boys. This was more than the original number of 45, and the reformatory had been recertificated for a maximum of 125. The inspection reports and the census returns show a steady growth, although with the traffic in and out, together with the variable number of boys out on licence, the numbers are approximate. From 1876 the reformatory seems to have operated at capacity.

To accommodate the rising numbers the buildings had to be adapted and enlarged, and an estate map in the possession of the present owners shows that the buildings had considerably outgrown Garnett's original tight square. As early as 1865 very considerable enlargement had taken place. In 1866 the inspector reported:

> the conversion of a large shed formerly used for industrial purposes into a school and dining room, the former schoolroom being made into a dormitory. The tailors' and shoemakers' workshops have been also enlarged, the laundry and oven better arranged, and another dormitory provided by the removal of the superintendent's office and a store room.[1]

In 1879: 'A new lavatory and a bath are much wanted.'[2] By 1880 a new lavatory had been constructed but: 'The dormitories are rather too closely packed.'[3] The bath was added in the same year, at Alfred King's request when he took over after his father's death. At some time separate staff cottages were built, and the master's house, still clearly identifiable from its handsome staircase and decorations, was on the other side of the square from that shown on the original plan. Local tradition still points to the shoemakers' workshop, outside the original complex, and from the evidence on the ground and on the map the original layout, with everything within a secure perimeter wall, was outgrown fairly early in the reformatory's life. The later reconstruction of the buildings into five cottages, as it remains today, makes it impossible to work out the exact changes.

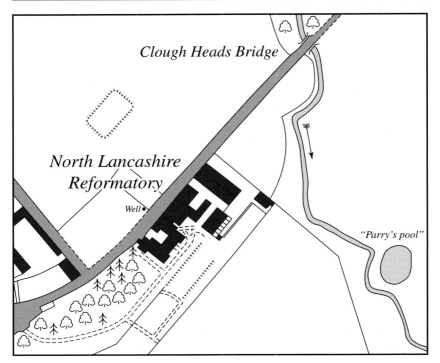

Clough Heads Bridge

North Lancashire
Reformatory

Well

"Parry's pool"

16: Bleasdale Buildings as Enlarged. Map drawn by Simon Chew.

By 1870 William James Garnett had relatively little direct contact with Bleasdale. Not only was his health failing, but he undertook other demanding responsibilities in public and private life. The reformatory was going along on an even keel, and Grant King was entirely reliable. As far as can be judged King wrote once a week, and the two men met fairly frequently when Garnett was in England, either at Bleasdale or by King driving over to Quernmore Park. For the first three months of 1870 Garnett was in the south of France; no letters have survived, but it may be indicative that there is no mention of Bleasdale in his diary during those months.

However, 1870 was to turn into a very bad year for the reformatory, a coincidence which is not entirely irrelevant. Returning from the south of France at the beginning of April, Garnett was almost immediately at loggerheads with Sydney Turner who sent out a questionnaire asking, amongst other things: 'How the school is supported and how the permanence of its management is secured.' Garnett answered stiffly:

> there can be no more guarantee for the permanence of its management than there has been for the last 13 years, which is my own life; when my son is old enough to help me, he may perhaps be disposed to do so, like Mr Baker's, but I can't be sure of this; I have no arrangements with the County, for they never required any; I never asked for any

money, and never received any from them, except for the maintenance of Inmates from one quarter to another.[4]

One could hardly ask for a better illustration of the up and down sides of much nineteenth century philanthropy, its private input into the public good, and its built-in impermanence.

As seen in Chapter 4, Turner's criticism of the dietary was rebuffed by Garnett with the statement about 'south country slops.' King also knew in 1870 that owing to rapid changes of staff the schooling was less than satisfactory, but Garnett took exception to Turner's remark on the subject: 'It is is however, not an uncommon thing that Managers and Superintendents see things in a different light from Inspectors.'[5] He refused to communicate further with him, and wrote instead to his deputy. The contretemps continued for a number of months, but peace was restored in the end, Garnett making amends: 'I have no desire to say anything offensive' but concluding his letter with a splendid example of how to have the last word. He had shown the correspondence to his brother-in-law, Edmund Moore Q.C. 'and he considered your letter .... but I won't say what, for I have no wish to keep up a sore subject, quite the contrary.'[6]

In June 1870 occurred the one event connected with Bleasdale Reformatory which remains in local memory after something approaching a century and a half; the drowning of a little boy, Edward Parry. Garnett was in London at the time, which was unfortunate for Grant King, but fortunate for us, as King sat down the same evening to pen a graphic letter:

> Today one of the most dreadful circumstances has happened: when the boys were going to the privies after breakfast at 9 o'clock, John Heyes came back and informed me that another lad called Parry had dirtied his clothes. I told him to take him to the pit on the moors and wash him. He took a bucket right enough and the boy's Sunday clothes to change him, but instead of washing him as ordered by me, he appears to have forced him into the water which is not deep. However the result was the death of poor Parry. Isaac Blackburn and his class were hoeing potatoes on the Moss, and I had no idea but that the poor lad was washed and had gone back to his class to Isaac till after 11 when a boy ran up to tell me that the lad was dead. I ran at once, but there was no hope. It appears that Heyes thought the boy was simply larking in the water, and so neglected him until it was too late.[7]

The inquest was a long and painful affair, ending in a verdict of misadventure, but with a strong rider 'that there was great carelessness by the authorities in not having proper inspection, and that the system of outdoor washing should be discontinued.'[8] The doctor's evidence

NORTH LANCASHIRE REFORMATORY, BLEASDALE, GARSTANG.

SCHOOL.   Meals, &c.

Clock } *Gilchrist*
Bell }
Mark Book   *Boles*
Master's Table   *Rushton & Gilchrist : Longley & Simpson*
   „ Books   *Smithson*
   „ Chair, &c.   *Haworth*
Stove –   *Stones*
Doors –   *Murray*
Medicine   *C. Garner*
Harmonium   *Ellison & Boles*
Tables –   *End boys*
Table Legs   *1 Boles 2 Gardner 3 Lu 4 Jno Johnson 5 Platt 6 Moss*
Bread   *Ellison, R Robinson Cunningham & Benson*
Baked Pudding   *ditto*
Milk } *Dennis Barry Rufook & Barns*
Potatoes } *Stead, Kennedy & Hodgkinson*
Porridge, Rice, Cocoa, } *Gilchrist Cunningham, Burgess Wrasly Farrer Cowell*
   Coffee, Soup, &c. } *Titterington, W Barnes. Rushton, Cottrill.*
Meat } *Ellison Brukell. R Robinson, Cunningham, Benson*
Cheese }
Water   *Ullershaw Earnshaw, Morewood*
Salt   *Gaffney*
Knives & Forks } *Hill*
Spoons }
Bones   *W Barnes*
Pigs Bucket   *Rushton & Hodgkinson . Fenton*

adduced drowning, but the circumstantial stories of the boys concerned – John Heyes who was in charge, and two others who were sent by Isaac Blackburn to see what was happening – suggest that cramp was also involved, and King himself believed this. The boys' evidence also indicated that Isaac Blackburn himself refused to have anything to do with that sort of punishment, and twice refused to get mixed up in it, sending boys instead to see what the trouble was – the first an 11-year-old.

Grant King himself was deeply upset because it came out in evidence that there had been a previous case when 'an excessive degree of cruelty had been used to a dirty – very dirty boy named Titterington by a man whom I had here for a few weeks on trial but whom I found unsuitable and dismissed at once.'[9] It was damning that he, the superintendent, had known nothing about that particular incident. It was damning that there seemed to be a lack of communication between the superintendent and his labour master:

17: Monitors' list, March 1870. Reproduced with the kind permission of the depositor and the County Archivist, Lancashire Record Office. Ref. DDQ/7/49/76.

8: Parry's Pool.
Photograph by
Angus Winchester,
2008.

I could only say that at all times such washing when it had been necessary was never intended as a punishment and that in cold weather it was done in the bath – but in warm weather as a rule at the brook or stream of water which runs by the Reformatory.

I stated the bare truth – I have at all times given such cases into the care of a man – he has had boys with him – but on Saturday, both Isaac Blackburn and I had too much faith in John Heyes – still I should not have sent the lad to the Moss – only to have him under the care of the Labour Master Isaac Blackburn – who certainly had the care of both boys and should have sent sooner to find out what was wrong. You can hardly imagine the state in which I have been since this occurred and especially since I heard of Day's misconduct which had never been reported in any way to me till this dreadful affair has happened.[10]

King promptly sacked Isaac Blackburn, a move of which Garnett did not approve but could do nothing about, since hiring and firing were exclusively in King's domain. Blackburn, who had been appointed as stockman in 1865, was reinstated a few weeks later and served the reformatory well for a number of years. Garnett came back from London and immediately drove over to Bleasdale:

Page 12.

BURIALS in the Parish of *Bleasdale*
in the County of *Lancaster*   in the Year 18*69*

Name.	Abode.	When buried.	Age.	By whom the Ceremony was performed
William Brotherton No. 89.	Goosnargh	May 8th	1 Year	R. C. Barclay
John Fawcett Fell No. 90.	Bleasdale	May 16-	8	R. C. Barclay
William Hunt No. 91.	Bleasdale	June 17.	26	R. C. Barclay
Richard Lawson No. 92.	Bleasdale	March 26th	1 Yr't	R. C. Barclay
Richard Edward Billington No. 93.	Bleasdale	May 17th	1 Yr't	R. C. Barclay
Edward Parry No. 94.	Bleasdale Reformatory	June 14th		R. C. Barclay
No. 95.				
No. 96.				

19: Admarsh Burial Register. Reproduced with the kind permission of the depositor and the County Archivist, Lancashire Record Office. Ref. PR 3237.

to see Mr King and how they all might be after their late distressing business; found all well and very happy to see me; walked out with GK to the Moss and to see the crops etc. and to see the pit where the poor boy was drowned.[11]

Garnett brought with him a letter which he had received from Jonathan Jackson, the much respected Quaker owner of the Calder Vale cotton mill, then in his 70s and foreman of the inquest jury:

On again and again revolving the subject over in my mind I am compelled to think that a grave censure does rest on the Governor of the Institution – Mr King in his evidence stated that he considered the deceased was being washed under the care of Isaac Blackburn the labour master, and Blackburn on his part says the lad was for that day under the care of the Shoemaker, and was washed by the lad Hayse under the direct orders of Mr King, he alone being responsible for it, and that when the cry for help was raised, he sent some of the boys, refusing to go himself saying (as one of the lads testified) "that since the case of a lad named Titterington he would have nothing to do or in any way be mixed up with such little washings." We were not allowed to enquire into this case of Titterington but I have since heard that great inhumanity was shown upon that occasion and Mr King stated that one of the masters had been discharged for it.

Although for the reasons I have stated we did not think this was a case of "manslaughter" nevertheless the solemn fact remains that the lad was drowned, and as this occurred so soon after the case of the lad Titterington and as I find that in Bleasdale there is a strong feeling that cruelty is often practised at the Institution, I do think it behoves those in authority (and I am very sure you will be anxious to do so as far as possible) to enquire into the facts of the case and if possible to remove the stigma which now rests on the Reformatory.[12]

King's response was to issue, through Garnett, an invitation to Mr Jackson or any of his friends to visit any time. 'Your visit too last Saturday was a great comfort to me. I hope now we shall again be able to go on in the same quiet way as hitherto.'[13] He had recovered his equilibrium, as the contents of the letter, and indeed the handwriting, clearly show: 'Your letter from town as to our getting to trust too much to our rules etc. etc. will not soon be forgotten by me.'[14] It is interesting to note that Garnett, originally the more rigid of the two, issued a warning, before he received Jackson's letter, about 'getting to trust too much in our rules.' It is equally interesting, from a modern perspective, to note that the inspector's annual visit happened to occur a week after the accident and merely noted: 'An unfortunate case of drowning took place in June. The circumstances of the case were carefully investigated. I think there was no sufficient foundation for imputing wilful negligence to the officers'[15] before passing on to more practical subjects.

However the inspector brushed over it at the time, the fact that this event is still remembered, the site of the pool still pointed out, indicates that the reformatory must to some extent have carried the stamp for the rest of its existence, although King could write a few days after the event:

> The foolish stories of cruelty etc so easily made up, will I have no doubt soon wear themselves out ..... I cannot think there are many who are enemies to us at the Reformatory, for whenever we want a kind neighbourly action done for us there is as a rule a ready response by most of the Bleasdale people.'[16]

All the local farms used reformatory boys at haymaking time, some of them employed boys on licence. There was every opportunity for information, accurate or exaggerated, to leak into the surrounding countryside. The relationship must always have been an equivocal one.

The third event had no public repercussions, and the reformatory's share in it was long past, but it must have rubbed salt into the wounds of that summer of 1870 when an ex-Bleasdale boy was hanged for murder.

Thomas Ratcliffe came from a part of Ince (near Wigan) called Hardybutts, a rough, tough place where nearly all the men worked down the pits from an early age. Thomas was no exception: on the 1861 census he described himself as a 'coal-miner'. He arrived at Bleasdale in August 1859, at the age of 13, having served his prison sentence in Kirkdale. It was probably immediately clear that he would be a handful, as Grant King, who at the beginning of July had wished to take 40 boys instead of the 32 he had, now wrote to Garnett: 'If possible we should again stop for a month or so as the last importations will want breaking in a little.'[17]

There is a four-year gap in the letters, but Ratcliffe turns up several times in Garnett's diary. In September 1861 he absconded but did not get far. Garnett recorded: 'Brought back by a farmer and I sent him off to Preston House of Correction for a fortnight.'[18] This was such an unusual response to absconding, which was normally dealt with in-house by a couple of days in the cell on short rations, that it looks as though it was the final, rather than the first, act of insubordination. Radcliffe was obviously a very difficult boy – not large, or powerful, indeed on the skinny side, but subject to wild and ungovernable rages. A year later he ran away again, and again did not get far: 'Ordered him to be flogged and kept in the cell till we thought fit. He is disposed to try to be master.'[19]

Radcliffe was now nearing the end of his sentence, but the next step was rarely easy. Indeed the struggle to find work placements was the most depressing aspect of Reformatory work: 'He wants to go into the army.'[20]

Unless Letters to Prisoners are marked as below, they will not be delivered to them.

DORSET COUNTY PRISON.

Direct to No. **11** *Thomas Ratcliffe*   Trial Ward, No. *1*

PRISONERS FOR TRIAL.

Persons writing to Prisoners in Dorchester Castle are to take Notice, that the permission to write and receive Letters is not given to Prisoners for the purpose of hearing the news of the day, but to keep up a correspondence with their relations, and to address them on the subject of their trials. They will not be allowed to give or receive any improper advice or hints, or to use or receive any unbecoming language.

It is therefore expected that their correspondents will not offend against the rules of the Prison in these respects. As all Letters sent into the Prison are read by the Governor, they ought not to be of unnecessary length.

All Letters or Parcels to Prisoners must be <u>carriage paid</u>, or they will not be taken in.

Dear Sir

This is the most ~~solment~~ solmaw moment of my life, I am now wateing for trial for stricking an officer with a spade so that he died eight weeks after, and when they held the inquest they brought me in Willful Mordor, for which I shall have to stand my trial at Dorset county syyeeas, friday the twenty second of July 1870.

20: Ratcliffe letter. Reproduced with the kind permission of the depositor and the County Archivist, Lancashire Record Office. Ref. DDQ/7/49/23.

Probably feeling that army discipline would be the best thing that could happen to him, Garnett went personally to Preston barracks to interview the Adjutant and try to get Ratcliffe taken as a recruit, but had no success.

In 1863–4, fairly worn out by the complications of his father's death and his own increasing ill-health (he gave up his parliamentary seat in the spring of 1863), Garnett spent a long winter in the south of France. King wrote very regularly and cheerfully, but his own workload was considerably increased by his manager's absence. In November he reported 'Ratcliffe [now 17] could not get work, and so on Sunday Oct 18 he returned here.'[21] In March:

> Foster took Ratcliffe to Lancaster to the recruiting sergeant and he enlisted him, but when he got to Manchester the Capt. would not admit him as he is too slender and there is some slight malformation of the backbone. So Ratcliffe is here again and must now think of work instead of fighting.[22]

The next plan was to send him abroad: 'I think it would be a good thing to send Ratcliffe to Canada on our own account; he will have a chance there and I feel convinced that he will be wrong almost immediately if we send him back to Wigan.'[23] In June Garnett noted: 'Went to Lpool a wet dismal day to see Ratcliffe and Moorby off to Canada.'[24] Ratcliffe came back, though history does not relate how long he was away. History does not relate anything until, in June 1870, Garnett received a letter from Dorchester Gaol:

> Dear Sir This is the most solnan moment of my life, I am now wateing for trial for stricking an officer with a spade so that he died eight weeks after, and when they held the inquest they brought me in Willful Mordor, for which I shall have to stand my trial at Dorset county syzeeas, friday the twenty-second of July 1870.
>
> God almighty knows what a life I have led since I left the school in 1863. And now look what has become of me hear I am between life and death wateing for my trial, may the lord defend me against my fows, I could not find it in my hart but to let you know the state I am in after all the advice you gave to me wile I was at that shool, but it is not too late to mend it ....
>
> Dear Sir, it is my temper and wicked toung that has got me in all this truble, I do not now what to do for I have nobody to take up my case yet.
>
> May the Lord work it for good that I may searve him in time to come. Amen
>
> Thomas Ratcliffe
Age 26, Born 1844, Aug 17th[25]

The prison chaplain saw this letter and wrote several times to Garnett, and probably others: 'in the hope that you may be able to render him some assistance in his distress.'[26] Radcliffe was already in jail and when out on a working party had attacked an officer with a spade. The chief witness was a fellow convict whom the chaplain felt might well have instigated the attack and then exaggerated its severity 'to escape his own present position by the sacrifice of Ratcliffe.'[27]

On his last morning, two days before his 24th birthday, Ratcliffe sent a message to Garnett by the chaplain: 'To you I was to say that he was grateful for all your kindness to him and that you had taught him the right way and that if he had taken your advice he would never have come to this.'[28]

Garnett recorded in his diary: 'This morning poor Ratcliffe hanged at Dorchester, may God have mercy on his poor soul.'[29]

The relationship between Garnett and Grant King was a close one, based on mutual trust and respect, though always within the bounds of mid-Victorian propriety. The social gulf was never overstepped – they worked together for 16 years, and to the end King addressed his manager 'Dear Sir' and concluded 'Your most obedient servant.' But there was nothing subservient: he was as anxious to share news of the things that went wrong as those that went right. When in 1867 he asked for a rise in his salary, the request was measured and dignified:

> I now wish to speak of my own affairs: it is now nearly ten years since I commenced work here, and I can not think you will feel I am exceeding my duty in any way if I respectfully ask for an increase of salary. Voluntarily I have advocated and you have allowed a gradual growth of the work both in the Farm, and the accommodation for boys and I do not believe there is one country Reformatory, except Kingswood, with an equal number of inmates where so little trouble is given either to the police or to the Inspector .... From my first coming here till now, I believe I have regarded the interests of the Reformatory as my own, and in every case, have striven as if for myself. But I need not say this to you, as from your uniform and confiding faith in my management I feel I could only be wrong to suppose you think otherwise.[30]

He did not add, which he might have done, that he was carrying more and more responsibility on his own. Garnett had been in the south of France since the end of January, after a month of ill-health, and four weeks after he left King mentioned that he had heard nothing directly, only through Thomas Cranston. However the request for a rise was answered with speed and generosity: his salary was raised from £100 to £150.

On the one occasion when they had a real disagreement, King's distress was very clear. It was in the autumn of 1870 – the year when so much went wrong. Probably, as may be adduced from Garnett's tetchiness with Sydney Turner, his temper suffered from the constraints of his disease and his own frustration with his ill-health. In October, Grant King had had some minor building alterations made without prior consultation, and promptly got a flea in his ear in return. But the apology is less that of a servant who has displeased his master and wants to justify himself, and more that of someone genuinely sorry to have upset a rather unpredictable friend, and willing to go the extra mile to make all smooth again. As always when King was disturbed, the handwriting is scrawly, the pen digging deep:

> I very much regret to find from your letter that you are not pleased with the arrangement I am making for the accommodation of the young man whom we hope to engage as schoolmaster .... You may depend upon this, that any alteration shall have your warrant before it is commenced in future. I hope, most sincerely, that no act of mine has ever shown in the least the least atom of disrespect to you. In addition to this, you have always expressed yourself so satisfied with me that perhaps I have omitted to consult you on some minor matters, where I certainly felt you would have sanctioned what I did.[31]

Two days later King wrote again, his pen under much better control. His tone was still conciliatory, but the alterations would remain as they were:

> I believe, though I am wrong in what I have done without your consent, still from the size and convenience of the new room you will, when it is quite finished and the furniture put in be thoroughly well pleased with the alteration .... I sincerely hope this office affair will never stand between us in the least as I should regret above all things to lose your good opinion, and especially your guidance and direction as Manager and I hope only Manager here.[32]

Garnett scribbled on the top that he had answered and fixed a visit. It all blew over and there is no evidence of any other difference of opinion in the two further years covered by Grant King's letters. The series stops at the end of February 1873, within a week of William James Garnett's last entry in his diary. Garnett died on 15 September 1873, and was buried in Quernmore churchyard on the 20th. Young William Garnett, at 22 the somewhat bemused inheritor of all his father's responsibilities, noted in his diary: 'A dark cloudy day fit for such a sad funeral .... Everybody was there and all were mourners.' Grant King contributed his own little sorrowful gesture. 'Each Reformatory boy threw into the grave as he passed a bit of mignonette. Bless them for their kindness.'[33]

In later years William Garnett ruthlessly pruned his accumulation of letters, but one year of Grant King's letters to him slipped through the net. It is that for 1874, when he was new to his responsibilities, but probably represents very fairly their relationship – which in fact did not differ much from the relationship with the elder Garnett in his declining years. Formally, William had been promoted from 'Master Willie' to 'Dear Sir'. His role as reformatory manager was almost entirely financial, even the agricultural side of the reformatory business being hardly mentioned. King had worked hard over the years to learn this side of his responsibilities; he read agricultural journals, he was surrounded by farmers, and he had had excellent personal tuition from Thomas Cranston. By 1874 he was confident in his own abilities, though Cranston was still at hand, visiting Bleasdale on estate business at least once a fortnight. Cranston may well have slept at the Reformatory, particularly in winter, as King, on his visits to Quernmore Park, frequently slept at the estate cottage. The 15-mile journey over the moor at Harris End was not to be lightly undertaken in an open gig on a dark wet night.

Young William Garnett had never been a scholar. The peripheral areas of music and sport had been his only areas of excellence at school and university. In many ways he had been a disappointment to a very demanding father, and this made him all the more determined to be a worthy successor. It would probably have been of advantage to give up some of his father's interests, but he took them all on in his early 20s: a not very mature young man struggling to come to terms with a life which was largely programmed for him. He was the owner of a 5,000-acre estate, the manager of a reformatory, the inheritor of his father's family and county relationships, and to some extent, the victim of well-meaning people who expressed their respect for the father by elevating the son to the same responsibilities: he was a magistrate at 23, and High Sheriff of Lancashire at 27. It is perhaps not surprising that the pressures built up over 50 years, and towards the end of his life he lurched from one nervous breakdown to another. At the beginning, from time to time his diary gives a glimpse into a troubled mind: 'Stayed for Holy Communion and felt better for it, ever so much. It does soothe anxious and overpowering thoughts.'[34] When he had sat as a magistrate for the first time: 'Hope to attend the Preston Sessions often and very regular so as to gain experience ..... It seems very cruel work though at the best; I pray that I may be always a merciful though a just magistrate.'[35]

His father's will had specifically allowed for the possibility of the reformatory being given up, but William opted to keep it, and with Grant King in charge, and although King's health was not as good as it had been, it was not a foolish choice. Between William James' death and his own marriage in 1876 he was away from home fairly often, staying with the Tatham family in Weybridge whose daughter, Bertha, he had decided to marry when she was 12 and he was 17. When he was at home,

IN MEMORIAM
GRANT KING
FOR 23 YEARS GOVERNOR OF THE
NORTH LANCASHIRE REFORMATORY
BLEASDALE
BORN MAY 3 1820
DIED JAN 26 1880
AND OF HIS WIFE
HANNAH KING
DIED JUNE 28 1911
IN HER 86TH YEAR

21: Grant King's memorial. Photograph by Angus Winchester, 2007.

William went with Cranston to Bleasdale at least once a month, as well as receiving regular reports from him which no doubt included information about the reformatory as well as the estate. A cursory reading of William's diaries might lead one to suppose that he had little real interest or time, since his Bleasdale visits covered the estate and the National School as well as the reformatory, but he was interested, though at one remove. There are no diary entries, as there is no written information from Grant King, about individual boys or the precise working of the place, but in February 1874 when he was at Weybridge, he talked with Henry Rogers 'the Reformatory man' (Sydney Turner's deputy and later replacement). He was also on the Diocesan Board of Education and reported his impression of his first meeting:

> A very charming and stirring day to me at least, to see earnest men doing their best to make good plans for the welfare of the people at large ..... May God in his goodness make me bear in mind the lesson I learnt, of doing good in my generation!!!³⁶

Grant King did not make old bones. He died on 26 January 1880 at the age of 60, after 23 years of unremitting and steadily increasing work.

In 1875 his son Alfred, who had been his father's assistant for six years, was appointed governor of the Liverpool Industrial School, his sister Emily going as matron. Isabella had earlier that year married Richard Gorst of the industrial school at Lostock Junction, so all three children, brought up in the reformatory and increasingly useful to their father as they grew up, left home, and Grant King's health deteriorated.

William Garnett felt the blow of King's death keenly: 'Had a telegram this day to say that poor dear Mr King died this afternoon. How dreadfully sad. The loss is dreadful. I little thought it would end like this. His family were all with him.'[37] It was towards the end of his shrieval year and he was in Liverpool for the Assizes, but made time for the funeral: 'After the funeral I had a chat with Alfred and he accepted the office vacated by the death of his father. Told him he would come on the same terms as his father had come, and also that I would give Mrs. King a pension.'[38]

The immediate result of Grant King's death was that the reformatory erupted in riot.[39] Alfred had gone back to Liverpool to sort out his position there, and the old familiar pattern had been rudely broken. A week after King's funeral the dormitory was unlocked at night with a stolen key, the boys rioted, the schoolmaster tried to intervene and found discretion the better part in the face of a score of burly 17-year-olds, about 20 of whom scaled the outer wall and took off for the fells. Fifteen were caught, three of them as far away as Southport. History does not relate what happened to the others but four ringleaders were brought before the local magistrates and sentenced to two months' hard labour.

It was an event that might have been foreseen. Facing the magistrates, the accused, who were all monitors, produced defences about too much beating. This was unconvincing, as Bleasdale was regularly commended for the rarity of its physical punishments. In both of the previous two years, the inspector had praised the system:

> The system of marks works well, and the way in which punishment is administered, except in grave cases, by fines, is worthy of more general imitation; by it, corporal punishment is to a great extent avoided, and the boys have a pecuniary interest in behaving well.[40]

It may well have been, in the highly-charged days since King's death, that the schoolteacher and labour master, who were left with the whole responsibility of what must have been an extremely volatile situation, had lashed out with their canes more than usual, but George Wilkinson, the instigator, had always been a difficult case. Since his arrival in 1875 he had absconded three times, and when he was licensed in 1879, he had promptly stolen again and gone to prison for 21 days. His behaviour in a maths lesson had been the flashpoint, moving from a sullen refusal to answer questions to throwing three slates at the schoolmaster and getting a cooling-off half hour in the cell as a result. But of course it was Grant

King's death, the sudden removal of the most enduring fixture in all their lives, which had made some kind of upheaval entirely predictable. Even with the removal of the chief troublemakers, and the arrival at the beginning of March of Alfred King as superintendent, it took time for equilibrium to be restored. The inspection was early that year, on 1 June, and the inspector reported

> The year has been marked by a good deal of absconding and disorder. I found matters mending at the date of my visit. The boys were then going on fairly well. Good discipline was gradually being restored.[41]

As far as can be judged from the inspector's reports, this was the last trauma in Bleasdale's history. The reformatory continued for another 25 years, and its even tenor must be attributed to Alfred King's superintendence, rather than to any real guidance from the new manager. In his early years William Garnett was by no means the worker his father had been. Although he took on the normal responsibilities of a country gentleman, in the early days of his marriage he enjoyed enormously the privileges of the life. The evidence of his diaries, which he kept faithfully, shows a man much more at ease shooting, fishing, 'archerising', skating, playing tennis, dancing, engaging in amateur dramatics, than anything else. However with increasing age he became more serious, and after the Local Government Act of 1888, when he was in his late 30s, he began to devote himself to its demands, and worked extremely hard, three or four days a week as a parish, district and county councillor, as well as a conscientious magistrate. He was particularly active in all matters relating to education, with the exception of his own reformatory. While he continued to support it financially and seems to have responded adequately or even generously to the need for building improvements which became more demanding as the years progressed and the acceptable standards of accommodation and hygiene rose, his relationship with Alfred King was ambivalent to say the least.

William Garnett had started out with every intention of replacing his father at Bleasdale, and was comfortable as long as Grant King lived, just as he was always comfortable with his agent Thomas Cranston, who did not die until 1911. Both were men of his father's generation, whom he had known since he was a child. But he suffered from a lack of confidence: as he grew older, he developed an extremely irascible temperament, standing on his dignity and barking rather than trying to understand another point of view. His diaries are peppered with angry outbursts at the unconscionable behaviour of his children, tenants, acquaintances, servants, political opponents, vicars, schoolmasters, and those who walked through his park without permission. He was conscientious, reliable and absolutely honest: he just could not cope with the behaviour of those who disagreed with him.

He was not a playboy and was sufficiently well-regarded in the wider world of reformatories to accept the position of President of the National Union of Reformatory Managers and Superintendents for 1884. He organised its preliminary conference in February of that year and stayed more than once at Hardwicke to confer with the aged and ailing Lloyd-Baker, who gave 'exceedingly clever advice.'[42] As the century progressed there was much discussion on the relationship between reformatories (controlled by the Home Office) and the industrial schools (controlled by the Board of Education). Garnett paid a number of visits to various establishments round the country, as well as having meetings on the subject with Alfred King and his brother-in-law Richard Gorst, who, as previously mentioned was superintendent of an industrial school at Lostock. But over the years enthusiasm cooled, and his visits to Bleasdale became less and less frequent (there are some diary years in which he records not a single visit). There must have been communication between him and Alfred King, but none of it has survived.

The trouble was simply that Alfred King got on very well on his own. The annual inspectors' reports certainly indicate that this was so. Bleasdale never failed to satisfy the inspectors, and King seems to have managed it with the same sensibly light but firm hand as his father had done. Nor did this go against Garnett's own philosophy. For several years in the 1880s the inspector (no longer Sydney Turner, who died in 1879) commented that the dormitories needed closer oversight: 'The dormitories are somewhat open to objection as not being under perfect supervision, but great care is exercised, and the utmost intelligence brought to bear upon the necessities of the situation.'[43] What the inspector actually had in mind is explained by a diary entry: 'The Inspector at his last visit tried to induce King to place peepholes in the dormitory doors. King absolutely refused and I am glad of it. The Inspector was obliged to give way at last.'[44] The disagreement was sorted several years later by some minor building changes.

The personal relationship between manager and superintendent may not have been comfortable, but it did not prevent Garnett responding to requests for building improvements as the following extracts from the inspector's reports show:

I found the whole establishment in excellent order, and very carefully and thoughtfully arranged. Improvements are introduced when the opportunity offers. The school moves with the times. It is not carried on in a sluggish routine without intelligence. When changes can be introduced they are carried out. The whole place in good working efficiency and under vigilant control.[45]

There is constant supervision and an anxious desire at all times to make the whole place practically more serviceable and efficient year by year. There are always some improvements to be found at every visit.[46]

On its own terms, therefore, Bleasdale seems to have worked well. It remains to try and assess how it measured up against other Lancashire reformatories and, in particular, with regard to the boys who were sentenced to its care.

Notes

[1]   Inspector of Reformatories, *Annual Report*, 1866.

[2]   Inspector of Reformatories, *Annual Report*, 1879.

[3]   Inspector of Reformatories, *Annual Report*, 1880.

[4]   WJG letter to S. Turner, LRO, DDQ 7/49/20.

[5]   S. Turner Letter to WJG, LRO DDX 7/49/20.

[6]   WJG Letter to S. Turner, LRO, DDQ 7/49/20.

[7]   GK Letter to WJG, 11 June 1870, LRO, DDQ 7/50/178.

[8]   Quoted in the *Preston Chronicle*, 14 June 1870.

[9]   GK Letter to WJG, 14 June 1870, LRO, DDQ 7/50/79.

[10] Ibid.

[11] WJG, *Diary*, 25 June 1870.

[12] J. Jackson Letter to WJG, 14 June 1870, LRO, DDQ 7/49/24.

[13] GK Letter to WJG, 28 June 1870, LRO, DDQ 7/50/182.

[14] Ibid.

[15] Inspector of Reformatories, *Annual Report*, 1871.

[16] GK Letter to WJG, 28 June 1870, LRO, DDQ 7/50/182.

[17] GK Letter to WJG, 10 Aug. 1859, LRO, DDQ 7/50.41.

[18] WJG, *Diary*, 6 Sept. 1861.

[19] WJG, *Diary*, 24 Dec. 1862.

[20] Ibid.

[21] GK Letter to WJG, 5 Nov. 1863, LRO, DDQ 7/50/43.

[22] GK Letter to WJG, 15 March 1864, LRO, DDQ 7/50/51.

[23] GK Letter to WJG, 8 April 1864, LRO, DDQ7/50/57.

[24] WJG, *Diary*, 9 June 1864.

[25] T. Radcliffe Letter to WJG, 17 Aug. 1870, LRO, DDQ 7/49/23.

[26] Rev. Lucas Watson Letters to WJG, LRO DDQ 7/49/23.

[27] Ibid.

[28] Ibid.

[29] WJG, *Diary*, 15 Aug. 1870.

[30] GK Letter to WJG, 28 March 1867, LRO, DDQ 7/50/11.

[31] GK Letter to WJG, 19 Oct. 1870, LRO DDQ 7/50/196.

[32] GK Letter to WJG, 21 Oct. 1870, LRO, DDQ 7/50/197.

[33] William Garnett, *Diary*, 20 Sept. 1873.

[34] William Garnett, *Diary*, 5 April 1874.

35   William Garnett, *Diary*, 23 Nov. 1874.

36   William Garnett, *Diary*, 9 April 1874.

37   William Garnett, *Diary*, 26 Jan. 1880.

38   William Garnett, *Diary*, 29 Jan. 1880.

39   *Preston Chronicle*, 28 Feb. 1880.

40   Inspector of Reformatories, *Annual Report*, 1878.

41   Inspector of Reformatories, *Annual Report*, 1881.

42   William Garnett, *Diary*, 8 June 1884.

43   Inspector of Reformatories, *Annual Report*, 1882.

44   William Garnett, *Diary*, 24 June 1881.

45   Inspector of Reformatories, *Annual Report*, 1889.

46   Inspector of Reformatories, *Annual Report*, 1895.

CHAPTER SIX

Bleasdale and Other Lancashire Reformatories: an appraisal

Open countryside, open air and home-produced food gave a reformatory like Bleasdale basic advantages over those in more confined spaces. So did the provision of hard but meaningful work. Under Alfred King the farm, which had shrunk in size in his father's later years, expanded to 160 acres, and the organisation of the boys' work was frequently praised by the inspectors, as was their appearance and attitude. 'Strong, robust, healthy,'[1] are the common adjectives used, as also phrases such as 'in good spirits, cheerful and contented.'[2] Bleasdale was not the only community to be described from time to time in similar terms, but it is fair to say that the inspectors were regularly struck by this aspect and thought it worth remarking on, as compared with their experience of other Lancashire reformatories. What is not known is how far the magistrates, in committing boys, exercised some form of selection in choosing those they thought most likely to benefit from a particular reformatory.

The system of rewards and fines had been favourably commented on many times since it was first introduced at the beginning. That it was thought worth explaining as late as 1890 shows that similar practice was by no means universal:

> A good system of marks works well. On first admission a boy begins to earn ½d a day; in his second year he earns, if his conduct remains good, 1d a day, monitors have 1d a day extra; fines are exacted for bad conduct, and there is very little corporal punishment.[3]

Perhaps even more illuminating of the philosophy is the remark: 'The mark list is posted where the boys can see it; the punishment list is not.'[4]

An advantage of the remoteness of Bleasdale was the variety of occupations which were possible, and which must have done much to vary the necessary monotony of reformatory life:

> Industrial Training. 18 boys were learning tailoring; 18 work in the shoemaker's shop. Most of the boys are employed about the farm and garden. The school authorities take contracts for roadmending. Turf is

22: Calder Vale Mill. Photograph by Angus Winchester, 2007. The old mill had no chimney during the period covered by this book.

cut in the neighbouring moors for fuel, and in the shooting season the boys are frequently employed as beaters. The boys form the greater part of the congregation of a small church in the neighbourhood. The superintendent is the vicar's churchwarden; the boys form the choir and undertake the duties of sexton, bell-ringers and clerk. The schoolmaster plays the organ.[5]

One can well imagine that going out with the keepers to beat the grouse moors was a sought-after chance to experience the outside world, as would be haymaking on the neighbouring farms and other work at busy times of year, for which the boys were extensively used. In evidence to the Committee on Reformatory and Industrial Schools in 1897 the Chief Constable of Preston referred to: 'such a place as Bleasdale, where the boys are really perfectly at liberty when they are on farm work.'[6] The same must have been true of those who worked as half-timers in the mill at Calder Vale. Whatever the official terms of engagement, and we do not know that they were particularly stringent, days spent away from the confined community must have been a positive experience, and we may further assume that some casual employers such as the shooting tenants were generous with small tips and treats. Roadmaking was severe work, as was the fact that much of the cultivated land was tilled by hand, but there was also a large cowhouse and dairy, horses, sheep and pigs, and many boys would have had experienced satisfaction in looking after animals.

How far this 'very good training for the colonies or country life'[7] was appropriate to the boys in question must remain a moot point, as by definition the vast majority came from an urban background, where their families still lived and worked. But for some it provided a good start in life. Sadly, it has been almost impossible, in spite of considerable effort, to trace individual histories of Bleasdale boys. The nineteenth century social ethos meant that most such personal histories were quietly forgotten, and until the 1890s, the fact that boys at the reformatory had first spent some days or weeks in prison resulting in what the Howard Association referred to as 'the "tarbrush" of the prison' led many magistrates to use the industrial schools instead. In his response to the Howard Association questionnaire, John Trevarthen, Secretary of the Farm School at Redhill, commented:

It is to my mind very striking that the enthusiasm and patient persistence of a few noble souls in the early days of the movement should have been so effective; and now, after many years conspicuous success, there is so little public interest taken in it, and indeed in some cases marvellous ignorance of the system which the magistrates have available in their hands.[8]

23: Clough Cottages: Bleasdale Reformatory now converted to housing. Photograph by Angus Winchester, 2007.

However, Lancashire appears not to have suffered from such ignorance, and the Chief Constable of Liverpool reported that: 'Magistrates in Liverpool are not reluctant to fully utilise Reformatory and Industrial schools.'[9] Bleasdale for one remained fully occupied until its closure.

Perhaps a not untypical boy was Thomas George Freeman, born at Willenhall near Wolverhampton in 1876, the youngest of six children. Both his parents died, and family tradition says that he was taken to live with his elder sister somewhere in the north-east. This proved an unhappy time and he ran away. What his offence was, or where he was sentenced, has not been discovered, but the 1891 census shows him at Bleasdale. The reformatory clearly served him well. He was better educated than his siblings, literate where they were not, and when his time was up he settled nearby in Chipping village, as a cowman. Thomas married a local girl in 1905, and brought up 11 children in a two-bedroomed cottage. He was a very worthy citizen and a pillar of Chipping church, where all his sons sang in the choir, establishing a family which was and remains in the third and fourth generation particularly strong in fraternal cohesion and support for each other. His 50 great-grandchildren have spread to Australia, New Zealand, Canada and Germany, and include doctors, teachers, farmers, policemen, soldiers, electricians and managers.[10]

For many boys the reformatory (local memory says that it was never called 'the reformatory', always 'the school') gave them a good start in life, and it is misleading to emphasise too strongly the severity of the conditions. By modern standards the conditions may be viewed as severe, but by the standards of the day they were deemed acceptable and the treatment of young criminals at Bleasdale may be compared with other establishments such as Ripley Hospital in Lancaster, opened in 1864 'for orphans and children of the indigent.'

Ripley was of course not a reformatory, and the children enjoyed a month's holiday in the summer, but for the other 11 months the regime was draconian. Boys and girls were strictly segregated – even in church they had to maintain 'eyes front' and refrain from looking across the aisle at the other sex. Brothers and sisters were not allowed to speak to each other and family visits were confined to three Monday afternoons in the year. The mixture of long school hours and physical labour, the conspicuous uniforms, the crowded dormitories of iron bedsteads with barely sufficient bedclothes, and the monotonous and ungenerous dietary, do not impress as treatment designed for children whose misfortunes were none of their own fault, and who were only received if they had been 'born in lawful wedlock, of poor and deserving parents', and guaranteed healthy. In some respects the Bleasdale boys were probably better off. Late in the twentieth century old pupils remembered the Ripley breakfast which was inevitably porridge without milk, the dinners (nothing but suet pudding on Thursdays, on Saturdays 'a thin soup with lumps of fat floating in it') and the scanty slices of bread for tea. It is also probable that there was much more reliance on physical punishment in the Hospital than the Reformatory. The first Principal, John Tyrer Preston, was definitely remembered as a 'strict disciplinarian who did not spare the rod.'[11]

Ideally, Bleasdale's performance should be compared with that of the five other Lancashire reformatories, but it is not easy to do this, as, with the exception of the Manchester and Salford Reformatory at Blackley, they were based on training ships in Liverpool.

The Blackley Reformatory was small, holding 40 or 50 boys. This makes it the more apparent that the first governor, Henry Antrobus, was something of a sadist. From the beginning he used a dark cell, chains and leg irons, which the committee agreed to in spite of their own reasonable 'Rules for the Governor' which instructed that punishment should be by 'Depriving of meals or any usual indulgence or by solitary confinement for a time not exceeding 24 hours.'[12] Antrobus lasted only two years. He was suspected of immoral conduct (reported by his schoolmaster). The committee cleared him, but they sacked him all the same. The government inspector cautiously noted 'I think that the committee have acted judiciously in accepting his resignation.'[13] Antrobus was replaced by Henry Arnold, one of the new type of professional reformatory workers, who had had several years of experience at Mary Carpenter's Kingswood. Arnold had a hard time trying to bring the place to order (there were 25 abscondings in his first 12 months) and the first year of his journal is notable for its complete absence of any apparent kindly feeling towards his boys. The most favourable comment he makes upon any boy is that: 'He does not require that amount of driving which the majority of them do.'[14] In 1863 the inspector commented: 'I found still a want of that kindliness of manner and consideration or sympathy towards the boys which are so essential to really successful management.'[15]

Things settled down and in many later years the inspectors found the place good enough ('62 boys looking, working and behaving well'[16]). But the committee was always desperate to make the place pay, and a large proportion of the boys' work was matchbox making which gave them neither satisfaction nor marketable skills. There were even years when they undertook oakum-picking – the soulless standby of jails and the inferior type of workhouse. The inspectors complained about this with monotonous regularity, but they had no powers of enforcement. It was a long way from the approving comment on Bleasdale at a later date: 'The lads are taught to turn their hands to anything that is practical and useful.'[17]

The training ship *Akbar* was, as has been said in a previous chapter, always something of a Liverpool showpiece and the inspectorate was – like the public – invariably impressed by the spotless physical condition of the ship. The educational achievement was also the best among the Lancashire reformatories, but the relationship between staff and boys was inconsistent from year to year, and varied very much from captain to captain. In 1863:

> The general aspect of the boys impressed me very favourably, much more so than the tone and manner of the men employed for their immediate superintendence and instruction, which seemed to me to be considerably more rough and hasty than is either necessary or advisable. The punishment book showed a large number of punishments during the year.[18]

However, three years later under another captain: 'The discipline of the ship is I think improved from Captain Borland's anxiety to have as little punishment, and to influence the boys as much by kindness as possible.'[19] *Akbar*'s darkest year was 1887, when discipline broke down completely. A mutiny in September resulted in ten boys being sent to Liverpool Assizes where the judge declined to punish them because he said it was all the fault of a feeble and inadequate staff. The ship was in need of complete reorganisation and a new commander.

None-the-less, in good times and bad, the captain's reports to the committee demonstrate that a steady trickle of boys had made good in the merchant navy or elsewhere, and wrote or visited their old school when their ships were in port, to report their continued good behaviour, and in numerous cases to show off the certificate which proved their promotion.

The Liverpool Farm School at Newton-le-Willows was established in 1859 as the *Akbar's* shore establishment. The site was not ideal, the available farming land being poor, crowded, and extremely expensive. However, the committee were fortunate in their appointment of a superintendent, R. H. Atty, who worked there until he died in harness in 1888, and was clearly one of the remarkable figures of the reformatory movement. At the top of his agenda was the development of trustworthiness in his boys, which meant that they were relatively free in school, and sent out on licence early. It took time for the system to work entirely satisfactorily, but the inspector consistently supported Atty's methods, and by 1865 his 'manly and straightforward system of training and personal disposition [has] succeeded in arousing a spirit of trustworthiness and exertion among the boys, and gaining the confidence of his neighbours.'[20] It is noticeable in the inspector's reports that Atty is frequently praised by name, which happened to no other except Grant King at Bleasdale. 'Mr Atty's system of trusting and trying the boys is fully justified by its good results ... The school stands among the first on my list.'[21]

In 1864 a second reformatory ship had been certificated. The *Clarence*, commissioned by the Liverpool Catholic Reformatory Association, was an old naval vessel first launched in 1827 and adapted for 250 boys. No official records of the early years of the *Clarence* appear to have survived, but from the inspector's reports it is clear that it was never among the more successful reformatories. The 1868 report commented that: 'the boys' conduct was generally good. Some of the officers had given trouble.'[22] In 1870 a sentiment was first expressed which over the years became almost an annual refrain – that any failures in the school were attributable to the poor quality of the material they were dealing with: 'With the rough class of boys he [Captain Algar] had to deal with, he found a necessity for repressing disorder with occasional severity.'[23] Given that the inspector visited for one day, or sometimes two, in each year, this criticism must have emanated from the ship's authorities, not from his own observation. On this occasion, his own observation was that: 'Some of the seamen instructors appeared to me to speak a good deal more roughly to the boys than the occasion required, a habit of no service to either party.'[24]

The inspector could admonish and encourage, and ultimately a certificate could have been rescinded, but short of that totally drastic step (and, were it taken, what happened to the boys under sentence?) he had no power beyond that of persuasion. *Clarence* continued to come bottom of the inspector's list among the Lancashire reformatories. In 1882 the ship's superintendent changed, with the consequent unrest which was normal, but in this case it continued for a full year, with 'cases of stabbing and wounding, gross insubordination, and violent conduct.'[25] On 17 January 1884 an arson attack burnt out the ship completely and six boys were each sentenced to five years in prison. The boys were removed to the now defunct Reformatory of Mount St. Bernard in Leicestershire, where, whatever their behaviour, their health improved dramatically.

The *Royal William* was commissioned to replace the *Clarence* in November 1885, and for a few years things improved. However, in 1892 the following comments were made: 'Some very vicious and depraved lads, requiring firm discipline and unhesitating resolution .... The lads admitted come from a violent and criminal class and need the firmest discipline.'[26] In July 1899 the ship was burnt out again, the boys moved to shore-based quarters in Flint, where there was a mass absconding on Christmas Day. It is said that by 1900 the officers were armed.

The *Clarence*'s shore-based other half, at Birkdale near Southport, held fewer boys and despite the healthier background of space, tended to mirror the ups and downs of the *Clarence*. Here also the staff emphasised, by way of explanation, the poor quality of the boys they received. This is interesting, since *Akbar*'s intake was also mostly from the rough end of Liverpool, and so was that of the Liverpool Farm School, which under Mr Atty was so notably civilised. The main difference was that most of the boys in the two Catholic establishments were from Irish immigrant families. Whether Irish families were really so much rougher than the indigenous stock, or whether there was something here of what we have come to call 'institutional racism' there is no means of knowing.

In the end, the reformatories have to be judged on their results. Those in Lancashire varied enormously in their treatment of their boys, and the skills with which they equipped them. How did they compare in their success at returning young men to the community, willing and able to live honestly and integrate into law-abiding society?

The second half of the nineteenth century saw a remarkable decline in both adult and juvenile crime, but how much of this can be attributed to the sharp focus on juvenile delinquency it is not possible to say. The 1884 Royal Commission on Reformatories and Industrial Schools produced some interesting figures. During a period in which the population had risen from 19 million to almost 25 million, juvenile commitments to prison, which would include boys sent to reformatories owing to the statutory preliminary prison sentence, fell dramatically:

1856	13,981
1866	9,356
1876	7,138
1881	5,483 [27]

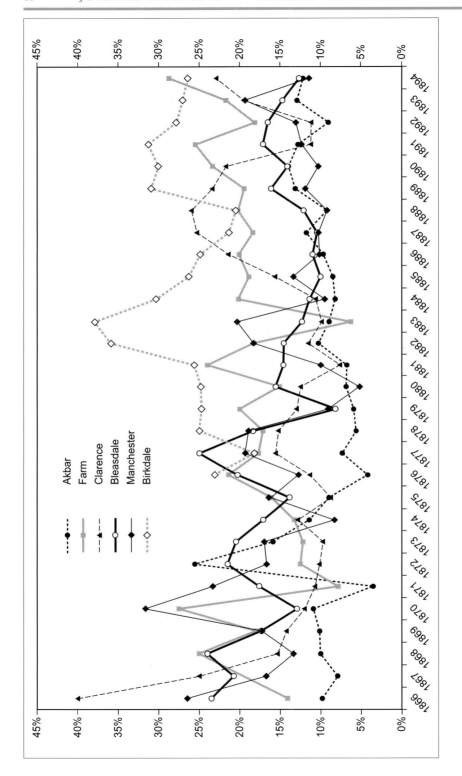

24: Relative Success Rates. Chart created by Mike Derbyshire and redrawn by Simon Chew.

The only available statistics which focus on the work of the Lancashire reformatories are those at the end of each of the inspector's reports, and these are not easy to interpret. The reformatories were required to return figures under six headings: the number discharged during the previous three years, those 'doing well', 'dead', 'doubtful', 'convicted of crime', 'unknown'. It is obvious that the returns were subjective and very much dependent on the reformatory's success in following up their boys, and this in its turn was dependent on the availability of staff and the emphasis which the establishment placed on their follow-up procedures. It has been noted that Bleasdale's failure in this respect in its early years was censured by Sydney Turner, but *Akbar* was the subject of an even more stinging rebuke:

> That so large a proportion of the boys discharged in the comparatively recent period to which the returns are limited, are unknown, seems to show great indifference as to what the results of the institution are, or great negligence in inquiring for them.[28]

With the possibility of records being so defective, as well as the procedure of collection over three years, meaning that some boys at the time of recording had been out a very short time, it is clear that the figures are questionable. The only real pointer to comparative success is the proportion of reconvictions, and this is unreliable not only for the foregoing reason, but because there is no proof that the reformatory would hear of all the cases. It seems most unlikely that there was any formal return from the courts – information would depend on the success of the institution's follow-up procedures, with additions, no doubt, from the inmates' own grapevine. However, something can be gathered and some trends noted. The figures from 1866 to 1894 are shown in Figure 24.

Akbar had a consistently low level of reconviction with only one sudden and unexpected rise, which is what one would expect when such a high proportion of its boys went to sea and were then under merchant navy discipline. It might be expected that the figures for *Clarence* would be equally low for the same reason, but the chart shows a very poor start and some significant rises. Birkdale, *Clarence's* shore-based subsidiary, was clearly the least successful of the six establishments on these figures. It is interesting to note that the Liverpool Farm School, so highly praised under Mr Atty for its standard of intelligent care, also had a significant tally of failures. Bleasdale was reasonably successful, more consistently under Alfred King than in his father's time.

Towards the end of the century the whole question of the treatment of juvenile delinquency was coming under scrutiny, well analysed by W. D. Morrison, chaplain at Wandsworth prison, in his book *Juvenile Offenders*

25: William Garnett aged 22 (private collection).

published in 1896, and the Howard Association's Report of 1898 which has already been referred to. This report began with a quotation from the *London Echo* which sums up a sense of alarm and anxiety very reminiscent of that of 100 years later:

> No one can have read the London, Liverpool, Birmingham, Manchester and Leeds papers and not know that the young street ruffian and prowler, with his heavy belt, treacherous knife and dangerous pistol, is among us .... The question .... is what is to be done with this new development of the city boy and the slum denizen.[29]

Both Morrison and the Howard Association saw a choice of four approaches to the problem, all of them with:

difficulties which have of late years been increased by change in public opinion and magisterial practice ….. Public opinion has in general disapproved the imprisonment of children …. [There is] a growing and well-founded feeling that the large number of commitments to costly Reformatories and Industrial Schools has often acted as an encouragement to reckless and drunken parents to endeavour to throw their offspring upon the honest taxpayer for support …. The infliction of whipping …. whilst finding advocates among many humane persons, is yet stoutly opposed by others, and has not found favour with Parliament ….. A recourse to fines (through frequent inability to pay them) leads to a majority of the actual imprisonment of children.[30]

The unresolved discussion continued into the twentieth century and beyond the scope of this study. The Lancashire reformatories, sea- and shore-based, were still well used and were adapted to conform to alterations in the treatment of juvenile delinquents. However, Bleasdale closed in 1905, and it is worth highlighting the circumstances of its closure, because these provide a relevant footnote to the developments during the 50 years of its life: the changes in public attitude to the problems of delinquent children, and particularly the change from the personal and highly individualised involvement of the mid-century gentleman philanthropists to the growing bureaucratisation of the treatment of juveniles. There were still private philanthropies, such as Dr. Barnardo's, but these were for the destitute, not the delinquent.

The immediate and obvious cause of the closure of Bleasdale was financial. The Garnett family fortunes were on a long slow decline, though the real crash did not come until 1920. William Garnett, catapulted into inheritance at an early age, had no experience of finance except that of running up debts at Oxford, which he had done enthusiastically in spite of his father's disapproval and his mother's pleading. Under his father's will he took on some heavy financial responsibilities, notably three sizeable annuities to his mother and two aunts, all of whom lived to a great age. The reformatory always needed support, and since the agricultural slump of the 1880s the possession of an estate was not necessarily the source of income it once had been. Garnett's excellent agent, Thomas Cranston, grew old and was succeeded by his son James, a far less efficient business man. Garnett's elder son had joined the Diplomatic Service, and continued to need a parental allowance; his younger son had not yet gone to Oxford; and there were three daughters.

In July 1904 Garnett wrote to the Lancashire County Council Finance Committee:

I find my Reformatory is costing me more than I care to be responsible for, even with every economy, and I shall be glad therefore if the

County could see its way to paying as from January 1st 1904 at the rate of 3/6 a head per week instead of 2/6 as heretofore. It is utterly impossible to keep my boys for less, our situation being as it is so far from all suppliers. I shall be glad if the Finance Committee can see its way to recommend this as I do not think it fair that I should personally any longer bear the responsibility.[31]

This request was refused. On 19 April 1905 Garnett made another plea for the extra shilling as the County 'have already granted it to Industrial Schools.' He also pointed out that he 'had never had any block grants made to me for buildings etc. as other schools have had, having made all such improvements out of my own pocket.'[32]

In fact Garnett had already laid the plans for closure, as his diary shows that on 20 March he had been up to London to see J. G. Legge the Inspector of Reformatories, and Sir Henry Cunningham at the Home Office, though he gives no details of the meetings. On 17 April, two days before his letter to the Finance Committee: 'At the Reformatory. Went through the stock with King and Cranston. Talked over with King the best way of getting all the boys transferred to other schools.'[33]

It is clear however that the real key to the closure was the ever more obvious alteration in balance between the manager who had little left to do except handle the private finance, and the superintendent whose responsibilities were now in almost all important matters directly between himself and officialdom:

Up to my reformatory at Bleasdale to say adieu to Mr and Mrs A. King, who are off on the 31st inst. I am breaking up the school, the Kings having got out of hand altogether. It was his school, not mine!! and has been so for some years. Only 10 boys now left, all the rest of the 125 being dispersed among other schools. Looked round with Cranston to prepare for the sale on the 11th. I shall be glad when I've seen the last of the Kings!![34]

A. King's last day at Bleasdale!!! My reformatory there, founded by my father, is now closed. Thank goodness! King was master! not servant! A great weight off my mind.[35]

The Bleasdale Reformatory served its original purpose well for 48 years, and finally fell a necessary victim to circumstances, having bridged in its lifetime a huge change in public attitude to the problem of juvenile delinquency, a problem which the twentieth century succeeded in solving no more conclusively than the nineteenth had done.

Notes

[1] Inspector of Reformatories, *Annual Report*, 1887.

[2] Inspector of Reformatories, *Annual Report*, 1890.

[3] Inspector of Reformatories, *Annual Report*, 1891.

[4] Inspector of Reformatories, *Annual Report*, 1888.

[5] Ibid.

[6] Howard Association, *Report on Juvenile Offenders*, 1898.

[7] Inspector of Reformatories, *Annual Report*, 1895.

[8] Howard Association, *Report on Juvenile Offenders*, 1898.

[9] Ibid.

[10] Information from Iris Westcott and Christine Whitehead, family descendants.

[11] Phythian, G., *The Ripley Legacy: Ripley St Thomas High School* (Ripley School, 1999).

[12] Minutes of Governors' Meetings, 21 May 1856, LRO, DDX 1791/1/1.

[13] Inspector of Reformatories, *Annual Report*, 1861.

[14] Governor's Journal May 1861, LRO, DDX 1791/5/4.

[15] Inspector of Reformatories, *Annual Report*, 1863.

[16] Inspector of Reformatories, *Annual Report*, 1868.

[17] Inspector of Reformatories, *Annual Report*, 1892.

[18] Inspector of Reformatories, *Annual Report*, 1863.

[19] Inspector of Reformatories, *Annual Report*, 1866.

[20] Inspector of Reformatories, *Annual Report*, 1865.

[21] Inspector of Reformatories, *Annual Report*, 1875.

[22] Inspector of Reformatories, *Annual Report*, 1868.

[23] Inspector of Reformatories, *Annual Report*, 1870.

[24] Ibid.

[25] Inspector of Reformatories, *Annual Report*, 1883.

[26] Inspector of Reformatories, *Annual Report*, 1892.

[27] Royal Commission on Reformatories and Industrial Schools, 1884.

[28] Inspector of Reformatories, *Annual Report*, 1871.

[29] *London Echo*, 7 March 1898.

[30] Howard Association, *Report on Juvenile Offenders*, 1898.

[31] Lancashire County Council, Finance Committee Minutes, 1904. LRO, DDX FLM/5.

[32] Lancashire County Council, Finance Committee Minutes, 1905. LRO, DDX FLM/5.

[33] William Garnett, *Diary*, 17 April 1905.

[34] William Garnett, *Diary*, 28 Aug. 1905.

[35] William Garnett, *Diary*, 31 Aug. 1905.

Bibliography

Manuscript Sources
Private Papers
Diaries of William James Garnett (1846–1873) and William Garnett (1873–1905). In private hands.

Lancashire Record Office
DDQ 7/50/1–266, Letters of Grant King to William James Garnett (1858–1873).
DDQ 8/21/136, Letters of Grant King to William Garnett (1874).
DDQ 7/46–9, William James Garnett: *Notes and correspondence* concerning Bleasdale Reformatory.
QGR 2/31-42, Rev. John Clay: Reports to visiting magistrates 1838–1855.
DDX 1791/5/1, Journal of the Governors of Manchester and Salford Reformatory.
DDX 824/1/1, Minutes of the Liverpool Juvenile Reformatory Association (1855–1863).
FLM/5, Lancashire County Council Financial Committee Minutes 1904–5.

Gloucestershire Archives
D3549/25/7/4, Lloyd-Baker, T.B.: Autobiography.
D3549/23/2/3, Reports on Hardwicke (1854–1869).

Theses
Jolly, S., *'A Manly Training to Obedience', Protestant Reformatories for Boys in Lancashire c.1854–1908*, Ph.D. thesis, University of Central Lancashire (2000).
Butterworth, J.C., *'The origin and early years of the Manchester Certified and Industrial Schools'*, Ph.D. thesis, University of Manchester (2000).

Parliamentary Papers
Reports of the Inspector of Reformatory Schools 1858–1895.
Report of the Royal Commission on Reformatories and Industrial Schools 1884.
Hansard Reports of Parliamentary Debates (1852–1857).

Newspapers

Lancaster Guardian (1854–1880).
Preston Chronicle (1854–1880).
Preston Guardian (1854–1880).
Illustrated London News (13 March 1847).
The Times (3 January 1854).
London Echo (7 March 1898).
Leeds Mercury (27 November 1854).

Other

Local information from A.G. Bengough, Jeremy Duckworth, Jean Fone, Sandra Jolly, Muriel Lord, Iris Westcott, Christine Whitehead.

Liverpool Record Office and Local History Service H285 MEL, Reports on Mason Street Reformatory School for Juvenile Delinquents 1856/7. Included in Melly, G., Stray Leaves, Vol. 1

Royal Philanthropic Society, Redhill, Surrey (1954), *The Story of the School 1788–1953*.

Annual Report to the Philanthropic Society, 1846.

Published Sources
Books

Briggs, A. (1963), *Victorian Cities* (Odhams Press, London).

Carlyle, T. (1850), *Model Prisons* (Latter Day Pamphlets).

Carpenter, M. (1851), *Reformatory Schools for the Children of the Perishing and Dangerous Classes* (Gilpin, London).

Dictionary of National Biography (Compact edn. 1975), Oxford University Press, Vols. 1 and 2, pp. 320, 383, 2367.

Clay, W.L. (1861), *The Prison Chaplain* (Macmillan, Cambridge/London).

Engels, F. (1845, 1st English edn. 1892), *The Condition of the Working Class in England* (Oxford University Press, Oxford).

Howard Association (1898), *Report on Juvenile Offenders* (Howard Association, London).

Morrison, W.D. (1896), *Juvenile Offenders* (T. Fisher Unwin, London).

Philips, H. and Verney, E. (eds.) (1889), *War with Crime* (Longmans Green, London).

Phythian, G. (1999), *The Ripley Legacy: Ripley St Thomas High School* (Ripley St. Thomas School, Lancaster).

Russell, C. (1917), *The Problem of Juvenile Crime* (Humphrey Milford O.U.P., London).

Victoria County History of Gloucestershire (1907), Vol. 2.

von Holtzendorff, Count (1878), *An English Country Squire as sketched at Hardwicke Court* (John Bellows, Gloucester).

Whiting, J. R. S. (1975), *Prison Reform in Gloucestershire* (Phillimore).

Articles

Duckworth, J.S., 'The Hardwicke Reformatory School', Bristol and Gloucester Archaeological Society, *Transactions,* CXIII, 1995, pp. 151–166.

Gerrard, B., 'Crime in Gloucestershire 1805–1833', *The Local Historian,* Vol. 35, No. 4, November 2005, pp. 219–229.

Gillis, J.R., 'The Evolution of Juvenile Delinquency in England 1890–1914', *Past and Present,* No. 67, May 1975, pp. 96–126.

King, P., 'The Rise of Juvenile Delinquency 1780–1841', *Past and Present,* No. 160, August 1998, pp. 116–166.

Index